I0554626

POSITIVE PROGRESS

IS MANIFESTING BULLSHIT?

CINDY WITTEMAN, KIMBERLEY WITTEMAN
& KAITLYN CHAVEZ

Table of Contents

The Authors

INTRODUCTION

This Mommy/Daughter trio will share their own life experiences of coming into abundance.

Within this book you will not only find true stories of triumph, but you will also find practical advice you can apply to your own life and circumstances to create the life of your dreams.

Cindy Witteman's growth from humble beginnings to becoming a TV Show Host, the Founder/CEO of a nonprofit, and Best-Selling Author is as extraordinary as it is motivational. In her chapters, you will read about how she started her life without resources and how she became successful. Was it Manifesting? Was it hard work? Was it complete bullshit?

Kimberley Witteman and Kaitlyn Witteman Chavez were born only 15 months apart, but their stories of struggle and triumph could not be more different. Each have written chapters that draw from their origins, struggles, and individual successes. Although they had a mother who taught them the core tenets of creating a life without limits from an early age, their stories of perseverance will inspire the reader as they forge their own paths from childhood to motherhood.

When Cindy first read about "Manifesting," she wanted to share the concepts with her daughters. Although mom had her own reservations, she told Kimberley and Kaitlyn about a movie she had seen that goes into details about and explains a concept known as "Manifesting." The girls watched the movie patiently and left the room thinking their mother had completely lost her mind with this "Manifesting" bullshit.

Fast forward almost 10 years later, they have set and achieved their own goals. They have created their own families and drawn upon the teachings of their mother to form their own individual beliefs and strategies. Now they have all come together as mothers in partnership to write this book and share their journey with the world.

Finally, they will share their own secrets while they answer the question that so many of us around the world keep asking: "Is Manifesting Bullshit?"

Cindy Witteman

Founder & CEO of Driving Single Parents, Inc., Host of Little Give TV Show & Owner of CFViews LLC

https://www.linkedin.com/in/cindy-witteman-a48851253
https://www.facebook.com/cindy.witt.902
https://www.instagram.com/cindy.witteman/
www.DrivingSingleParents.org
www.LittleGive.com
www.CFViews.com

My Name is Cindy Witteman. I am a Business Owner, Best Selling Author, TV Show Host, Entrepreneur, Nonprofit Startup Coach, Speaker, Beekeeper, and the Founder/CEO of Driving Single Parents, Inc. I am a former single parent and proud stepmom with six kids, one grandson, and two granddaughters. I enjoy traveling, spending time with family, and helping others see the positives in life. I have a passion for giving back and helping single parents regain their independence. In 2017, I founded Driving Single Parents, Inc., a nonprofit that recently celebrated six years. Through hard work and dedication, we have changed the lives of multiple single-parent families by providing them with reliable vehicles at NO cost to them. These vehicles have given them the ability to transform their struggles into a thing of the past. To learn more, visit DrivingSingleParents.org. To learn more about the *Little Give TV Show*, visit LittleGive.com.

INTRODUCING A JOURNEY OF TRANSFORMATION: FROM STRUGGLE TO ABUNDANCE

Life often presents us with challenges that seem insurmountable, leading us to feel that we are trapped in circumstances beyond our control. However, the remarkable journey recounted here challenges that notion, offering a profound exploration of how we can harness our minds' power to break free from limitations and create a life of abundance. This narrative invites you to step into a world where manifesting, gratitude, and purpose converge to pave the way for a transformative experience.

In the following chapters, you'll embark on a captivating voyage that traces the evolution of a life marked by financial constraints, self-doubt, and perpetual struggle. Through a candid account of setbacks and resilience, the author unveils the layers of her personal journey, revealing how the mind can be both a prison and the key to liberation. From childhood memories of lack to the challenges of single motherhood, the narrative candidly explores the hurdles that once defined the author's reality.

As you delve deeper into the pages, you'll witness the pivotal moments that sparked a shift in perspective—a realization that the mind's capacity knows no bounds and that the keys to abundance lie within reach. The journey unfolds through the lens of manifesting, where dreams are transformed into reality through a combination of positive thinking, deliberate action, and an unwavering commitment to change. The author's experiences serve as a guide, demonstrating how the power of thought, when harnessed correctly, can manifest profound shifts in one's circumstances.

With a focus on actionable steps, the narrative explores the journey toward transforming negative thought patterns into a reservoir of positivity. The concept of gratitude emerges as a driving force, as the author navigates the path from scarcity to appreciation, gradually reframing her perception of what is possible. Through introspection and self-discovery, you'll witness the birth of a renewed sense of purpose—an inner fire that propels the author forward, enabling her to navigate the challenges of life with newfound clarity and determination.

The pages that follow invite you to journey alongside the author as she unravels the mysteries of manifestation, gratitude, and action. With each chapter, you'll gain insights into practical techniques and transformative mindsets that have the potential to unlock your own journey toward abundance. Prepare to be inspired, motivated, and empowered as you learn from the author's remarkable voyage from struggle to a life enriched with promise and possibilities.

CHAPTER 1
IS MANIFESTING BULLSHIT?

Manifesting, often dismissed as mere wishful thinking, is in fact far from nonsense. The essence of my journey into abundance unveils the astonishing power of the mind—a realm that continually eludes comprehension. This journey proves that boundaries are figments of our imagination, and the only limits that exist are those we construct for ourselves.

Throughout my life, I've been plagued by a sense of confinement, as if trapped within the constraints of circumstances. However, a point came at which a profound epiphany dawned on me—my mind, being extremely intricate, was both the prisoner and the jailer. This revelation opened my eyes to the fact that the key to liberation was within reach, hidden in plain sight all along. I had inadvertently confined myself within the walls of my own thoughts. But now, having seized that elusive key, I am determined to guide YOU in unlocking your own prison door, so you can stride into a life brimming with potential and countless possibilities.

"Rooted Beginnings: Unveiling the Heart of My Story"

Emerging from a childhood marked by financial struggles, I found myself situated on the lower end of the economic spectrum. The basics that many take for granted were elusive to me. While my mother possessed a desire to provide for us and shield us from want, her own disabilities, self-imposed limitations, and the challenges she faced as a single parent hindered her efforts. Despite her aspirations to elevate our circumstances and become a more substantial provider, she faced insurmountable barriers. Consequently, moments of scarcity, including the absence of essential amenities and reliable transportation, frequently characterized our existence.

My memories include perpetual apprehension about the imminent disconnection of electricity or water services. I distinctly recall instances when our vehicles were repossessed, comprehending the implications of this even at a tender age. Evictions were not uncommon, and returning home to discover new locks on the door due to unpaid bills was distressingly familiar. These circumstances often led to the forfeiture of my childhood possessions, as the landlord withheld our belongings until payment was rendered—an impossibility given our dire financial state. I vividly remember rummaging through discarded items in search of my toys and clothing. At times, we stumbled upon discarded belongings from others, which occasionally surpassed the quality of my own.

As I grew older, it became clear to me that our challenges weren't common to everyone. This realization motivated me to initiate conversations with strangers, fueled by a natural curiosity to unveil the stories behind their ownership of nice clothing, cars, and houses. Deep within me, a fear of scarcity had taken root, a persistent worry that whatever I had could vanish unexpectedly.

Marriage seemed like a way out of the poverty and bleak financial circumstances I faced while living with my mother. I believed that by getting married at a young age, I could escape the challenges I was living with. Unfortunately, this decision only led me from one unfavorable situation to another. After marrying, I swiftly became a mother to a daughter, and over the next dozen years, I welcomed three more daughters into my life. My focus shifted entirely to caring for my children, and I expended an excessive amount of energy attempting to mend the lives of those around me.

Eventually, I found myself leaving that marriage, entering the realm of single motherhood, and becoming the sole provider for my family. This transition, however, left me in a never-ending cycle of scarcity. To keep the lights on, I had no choice but to juggle two jobs. I recognized that unless I found a way to elevate myself from this struggle, I would be tethered to multiple jobs for the rest of my days. Determined to break free, I embarked on a quest for stability, driven by the desire for my daughters to view me as a role model. This aspiration led me to pursue further education, with the hope that I could eventually be secure in a career that would exceed the confines of my current situation.

Inspired by medical dramas like *ER*, I set my sights on becoming a nurse, convinced that it would be a path that would make my daughters proud. However, reality struck me hard—I despised nursing. Once again, I found myself in a scenario where I was pushing against resistance, expending energy, and merely spinning my wheels in an attempt to attain a version of success that would impress others.

After leaving nursing, I transitioned to a corporate job that demanded a minimum of 50 hours per week. This further distanced me from my daughters, prompting my father to intervene. He candidly explained that if I remained on this trajectory, my daughters would grow up with a mother they hardly knew. He shared this insight with a level of concern that ignited a turning point. Fueled by my father's wisdom, I took a leap of faith and ventured into the legal field. Despite the substantial pay cut this shift entailed, it turned out to be one of the best decisions I've ever made. In retrospect, my gratitude towards my father for this invaluable advice knows no bounds.

Yet, throughout this tumultuous journey, one element remained strikingly absent: consideration for my own desires. My life had been dominated by a constant state of fight, flight, or survival mode. My efforts were directed toward impressing my father and daughters, and I focused just on getting through each day. The result was a life lived on autopilot, without passion and genuine fulfillment. I was no stranger to engaging in harsh self-dialogue, berating myself for perceived inadequacies and stagnation in both my personal and professional realms. My attempts at self-improvement were marred by self-sabotage, as I adhered to a course of action dictated by external expectations rather than pursuing what truly resonated with me. My relationships, too, reflected this pattern—I often found myself attempting to reshape others to fit into my life, rather than seeking individuals who naturally complemented my journey.

A Glimmer of Hope:

As life progressed, I gradually recognized that my pervasive feelings of lack and fear were serving as barriers to embracing abundance. An intriguing moment of revelation came when I encountered a movie and book, featured on the Oprah Winfrey show, called *The Secret,* by Rhonda Byrne. Initially, I scoffed at the idea that anyone could believe in what I deemed to be such absurd concepts. Skepticism led me to dismiss the book and its teachings as mere nonsense.

However, by 2013, I found myself grappling with the overwhelming challenge of improving my circumstances. I began to consider revisiting *The Secret.* The repetitive cycle of ending up in the same difficult situations despite my efforts pushed me to a breaking point. Desperation compelled me to give *The Secret* a chance. As a single mother, I had resorted to selling plasma twice a week just to keep up with bills and provide for my daughters. It was against this backdrop that I leaned into the teachings of *The Secret.*

Unveiling the Mystery: Is Manifestation Actually Real?

Consider the parallels between the unseen forces of natural phenomena such as electricity and gravity and the idea of manifesting. While we can't physically perceive energy, we experience its effects, such as feeling a shock when coming into contact with electricity. Similarly, gravity's presence is evident through the way objects fall.

Manifestation operates on the premise that our thoughts and intentions might attract what we desire, even if we don't fully comprehend the mechanics behind it. Just like an electrical outlet, even if we don't understand its intricacies, manifestation could potentially work in ways beyond our current understanding. By directing our focus and energy toward our goals, could we be tapping into this hidden force and influencing the course of our lives?

Embracing "The Secret:" Unveiling the Power Within

Following *The Secret's* teachings meticulously, I wrote blank checks to myself, embellished my bank statement with extra zeros, adopted a gratitude rock, envisioned myself driving my dream car, and even crafted a vision board adorned with images of my desires.

Not So EASY!

Navigating this path was far from simple. I spent months employing these strategies, focusing intently on manifesting. Yet, disappointingly, not even the smallest change manifested in my life. In frustration, I threw in the towel, berating myself for wasting energy on what seemed to be an empty pursuit. That blank check was torn apart, the vision board dismantled, and the once-prized gratitude rock discarded in a nearby pond. My perception grew darker; a series of negative circumstances appeared to flood my life. Bills mounted, income stagnated, and adversity seemed relentless.

Yet, the turning point arrived at the close of 2013. Driven by desperation, I turned to the Audible versions of *Think and Grow Rich* and *The Secret*, listening with renewed intent. Determined for change, I crafted a New Year's resolution for 2014, vowing to embrace the teachings of these materials, but with a new focus. Rather than seeking a radical transformation of my entire reality, I aimed to shift my mindset toward positivity. Gratitude for my existing blessings, self-compassion, and the act of articulating my aspirations were the new pillars I sought to build upon.

This marked a juncture at which I granted myself permission to introspect and pen down my thoughts, hopes, and dreams—a previously uncharted endeavor. While I could readily outline others' desires, my own remained elusive. Gazing into my own desires felt like staring at a blank canvas. To bridge this gap, I channeled my energy into gratitude, acknowledging even the seemingly modest aspects of my life.

The magic of consistent writing soon began to unfold. Each night, words flowed from my mind onto paper, slowly crystallizing into my goals and aspirations. As my nightly writing sessions continued, the murkiness surrounding my dreams lifted. Gratitude became a morning ritual, and a newfound sense of hope began to emerge, subtly shifting my perspective in a more positive direction. Although no shiny new car appeared in my driveway, the transformation was internal and profound.

My inner dialogue shifted from self-criticism to empowerment, allowing me to recognize my achievements—a custom-built four-bedroom house, a fulfilling job with benefits, and the strength to raise four children alone. The realization dawned on me—these accomplishments had been present all along, obscured by my inability to recognize and celebrate them. This shift in perspective initiated a cascade of change. My career surged forward, friendships deepened, and even my dating life underwent a remarkable shift. I let go of settling for attractive yet flawed partners, prioritizing my own desires instead.

An epiphany emerged: The power to shape my future had always been within me. The narrative of my life was mine to compose. The mist of uncertainty parted, revealing a future illuminated by sunshine and limitless possibilities. Through a simple choice to alter my outlook, I discovered the profound potential of personal agency and the transformative impact it could have.

Vision Board

Embracing a new chapter of empowerment, I created a fresh vision board adorned with images that painted a vibrant tapestry of my aspirations. Travel, robust health, unwavering financial stability, and exhilarating new ventures found their place on this visual representation of my dreams. Each day, I devoted time to gazing upon this collage, allowing my mind to dance through the scenes and possibilities it depicted.

This ritual became a bridge between my dreams and my reality, guiding me to contemplate actionable steps that could propel me toward these goals. No longer a passive observer of my own desires, I had harnessed the momentum to actively shape my future. This vision board became more than a collection of images; it evolved into a compass pointing me in the direction of my passions, inspiring a pursuit of tangible progress.

Turning Point

In a profound turning point, my journey through reading, self-discovery, and deepening knowledge about manifesting unveiled a pivotal truth: Abundance wasn't solely about amassing wealth, but rather about mastering the art of making the most out of the resources at hand. Given my personal struggles through financial scarcity, domestic adversity, single parenthood, and various other trials, I resolved to shift my focus from manifesting money to giving back and supporting others.

Guided by empathy, I sought ways to aid fellow single parents who were grappling with challenges similar to those I had experienced. Recognizing that I couldn't single-handedly unravel all their complexities, I still understood that every small gesture of assistance held the potential to make a substantial impact on their lives.

Refining my mental landscape became a cornerstone of this transformation. Purposefully, I nurtured a mindset oriented towards positivity and solutions, redirecting my energy from fixating on problems to envisioning ways to overcome them. I consciously refrained from vocalizing minor setbacks, recognizing that voicing negativity granted it power, both over myself and those who heard it. By stopping the cycle of negativity, I prevented bringing more of what I didn't want into my life.

By embracing gratitude and staying positive, a remarkable change happened. This shift in perspective led to a rapid influx of positivity, reshaping my reality and showing me how our outlook impacts our experiences.

Stop Worrying

Overcoming the hurdle of incessant worrying was a pivotal step in my journey. The weight of my past experiences had etched into me an unhealthy habit of incessant worry. Each potential outcome, every potential hurdle that hadn't yet materialized, would flood my mind with anxiety. I was, in essence, a walking ball of fear and stress. As I embraced positive thinking, I realized how pointless excessive worrying was.

My mind, once a racetrack of thoughts darting in every conceivable direction, now hinged on the situation at hand. I stopped worrying about every possible mistake and started living in the moment. If a situation did unravel unfavorably, I confronted it head-on, concentrating solely on solutions for that particular predicament. Remarkably, the decision to relinquish worry began to yield tangible effects—I felt a lightness, a liberation from the shackles of stress that had once gripped me so tightly.

With every ounce of intent, I steered my mind away from that bottomless pit of worry, and the transformation was staggering. A weight that had burdened me for so long, one that had siphoned 90% of my emotional energy, began to lift, unveiling the immense power that could be harnessed by simply choosing not to worry.

Action Action Action

Certainly, the misconception that manifesting is solely about wishful thinking is far from accurate. Although visualizing and believing are crucial, they form the groundwork upon which action must be built. Think of them as the blueprint for a magnificent structure—essential, but not sufficient on their own.

Manifestation isn't a magical shortcut; it's a dynamic interplay between your thoughts and your actions. Consider a scenario where your aspiration is to complete a marathon. While adding this goal to your vision board is a positive step, it's merely the spark. To turn this aspiration into reality, you must engage in deliberate planning and put forth actionable measures. The marathon won't unfold at your doorstep without your active involvement.

Your path to abundance hinges on bridging the gap between thought and action. Your ability to translate your thoughts into tangible efforts holds the key. While dreaming is your starting point, it's the deliberate pursuit of those dreams through consistent action that turns the abstract into the concrete. The journey of manifestation doesn't conclude with mere contemplation; it reaches its climax as you steadfastly stride towards your objectives.

Write it Down

When you write down your dreams and goals, you're essentially giving your thoughts a tangible form. The act of putting pen to paper or typing them out on a screen brings a level of clarity and commitment that mere contemplation lacks. It's like giving your thoughts a concrete shape, making them more real and achievable. Your written goals become a roadmap that your subconscious mind can follow, helping you stay on track and work towards them.

Crafting a Vision Board

A vision board takes this visualization a step further. By gathering images, words, and symbols that represent your goals and desires, you're creating a visual representation of your dreams. Placing this board somewhere you'll see it regularly keeps your goals at the forefront of your mind. It's like embedding a constant reminder in your consciousness, which triggers your subconscious to actively seek opportunities, connections, and actions that align with your vision.

Verbalizing Your Ambitions

Another powerful technique. When you speak about your goals, you're not only sharing your intentions with others, you're also reinforcing them within yourself. The spoken word carries a certain weight and commitment that can motivate you to take action. Moreover, talking about your goals with others can attract like-minded individuals, mentors, or collaborators who can provide guidance, support, and valuable connections.

Harnessing the Power of Your Subconscious Mind

Writing, creating, and speaking engage your subconscious mind in a focused and directed manner. Your subconscious is always working behind the scenes, processing information and seeking ways to make your thoughts a reality. By consistently feeding it with your aspirations and desires, you're effectively programming it to help you achieve your goals. Whether your dreams are big or small, simple or complex, your subconscious mind will be your ally in making them come true.

As you jot down your dreams and delve into their intricacies, your brain gets to work. It starts to create avenues, carving out routes to bring your aspirations to life. Throughout this process you'll notice an alignment of ideas, individuals, and opportunities in your life. These newfound connections serve as tools to elevate your thoughts and concepts to the next level.

How Your Mind Transforms Desires into Reality

The Power of One More by Ed Mylett vividly demonstrates this concept. Consider desiring a blue van—once this thought occupies your mind, you'll begin noticing blue vans in places where they previously escaped your attention. Your brain discerns relevance and compels you to focus on these pertinent elements. Similarly, when you contemplate launching a new business, your mind hones in on aspects pertinent to achieving this objective. While you generate many thoughts daily, your brain streamlines its processes, filtering out irrelevant thoughts. Upon training your mind to align with your objectives, formerly disregarded elements resurface prominently, guiding you toward your goals.

Don't Wait for a Miracle

It's crucial to acknowledge that manifesting necessitates more than passively waiting for miracles. Even lottery winners must purchase their tickets. Dreams remain unrealized without action. Once you identify your true desires, you can initiate the process of manifestation, encouraging your mind to highlight relevant opportunities. Subsequently, taking action based on these insights tilts the scales of life in your favor.

Avoid Overwhelm

Remember, fixating solely on the steep climb ahead can be overwhelming. Instead, focus on taking incremental actions, one step at a time. This approach ensures steady progress towards your dreams. By consistently moving forward, you naturally inch closer to the summit of your goals, achieving positive outcomes.

It Is Easy to Dream and Hard to Apply

Indeed, envisioning a better scenario is far simpler than putting those visions into practice. Human nature often finds us wrestling with habits that hinder progress, even when the solutions seem straightforward. Take the classic example of someone frustrated by morning rush and tardiness. They readily acknowledge the root cause and recognize the remedy: waking up earlier to alleviate stress and punctuality issues. Yet, the next day arrives, the alarm buzzes, and they smack that snooze button once again, perpetuating the same cycle.

It's perplexing why many individuals hesitate to act, especially when the solutions appear evident. Many times, the tools to resolve these dilemmas are literally at their fingertips, ready for utilization. Despite knowing the steps required to make positive changes, a barrier seems to arise between intention and action.

People often stick to habits even if they're harmful, because they feel familiar and safe. Our minds often choose what's easy now over what's better in the future. This can make us ignore better options in exchange for short-term comfort.

Change also requires effort and discipline, both of which can be challenging to do consistently. The discomfort of transition, the fear of failure or an unknown outcome might contribute to this resistance. Motivation can wane when faced with obstacles, leading to the persistence of status quo.

Overcoming this involves a shift in mindset and a concerted effort to bridge the gap between intent and action. It might require techniques like setting clear, achievable goals, creating actionable plans, and enlisting accountability partners. Cultivating self-awareness about the triggers of inaction and seeking motivation can also be powerful tools.

In essence, acknowledging a problem is merely the first step, and it's the subsequent consistent actions that truly propel change.

Encouragingly, even the simplest adjustments can lead to profound transformations if met with commitment.

Stop Spending So Much Time-Wasting Time

CoCo Chanel's analogy perfectly captures the sense of futility that comes with wasting time in unproductive loops—it can feel like banging one's head against a wall, hoping it will miraculously transform into a door. For years, I found myself working tirelessly, exerting force, and attempting to make things happen without achieving the desired results. It was like squeezing through a tiny rabbit hole instead of recognizing the array of open doors available.

The realization that manifestation offers a different approach, one without the need for force or struggle, opened me up to a new perspective. It's akin to turning around to discover an entire hallway full of open doors, each representing new opportunities waiting to be explored. Often, our actions are dictated by our beliefs, even if they go unquestioned. For instance, if presented with a locked door, some might stay confined based solely on their belief that it's locked, without attempting to open it.

Navigating the journey of manifestation requires emotional mastery. While problems and setbacks are inevitable, your mindset shifts from treating them as barriers to seeing them as mere bumps in the road. Managing your emotions becomes paramount. It's not about pretending to have a perfect life but rather dealing with negative emotions constructively and promptly shifting to positive thoughts. Just as you change the channel on TV to avoid a show you dislike, you can switch your thought patterns. When negativity creeps in, change the mental channel—recall happy memories, reach out to a friend, or focus on positive aspects.

This practice of "changing the channel" becomes a powerful tool to halt the downward spiral of negative thoughts. Over time, with consistent effort, your mind becomes adept at switching to positive perspectives automatically. This shift empowers you to maintain emotional equilibrium and remain resilient in the face of challenges.

By embracing this mindset, you transition from forcing outcomes to allowing opportunities. You free yourself from the wall-banging struggle and instead stride confidently through the open doors that present themselves on your path to growth and abundance.

The Importance of Feeling Good

The way we feel and the perspectives we hold play a significant role in shaping our experiences and overall wellbeing. When you encounter someone who exudes positivity, sees the silver lining in most situations, and uplifts those around them, you witness a person who is truly content and leading a fulfilling life. On the other hand, an individual who is perpetually negative, complains about external circumstances, and carries an aura of anger is reflective of someone who is trapped in misery and unable to embrace the joys of life.

Remarkably, both these paths are products of our thoughts and choices. If you find yourself in a cycle of stress, worry, and fear, it becomes challenging to fully engage with life's richness and potential. To unlock greater fulfillment, it's essential to seek ways to cultivate feelings of joy and gratitude.

Choosing to approach life with positivity doesn't mean ignoring challenges or pretending that everything is perfect. Instead, it's about framing situations in a way that empowers you to navigate difficulties and setbacks more effectively. By maintaining a mindset focused on joy and gratitude, you create a foundation for growth, resilience, and a heightened sense of wellbeing.

Ultimately, the journey to a more abundant and satisfying life starts within you. Your thoughts and emotional states have a profound impact on your experiences. By consciously steering your thoughts toward positivity, gratitude, and joy, you are not only enhancing your own wellbeing but also influencing the world around you in powerful and uplifting ways.

Purpose

Certainly, discovering and embracing your sense of purpose is a transformative journey that holds the potential to shape every aspect of your life. It's a process that involves delving deep within yourself, exploring your passions, values, strengths, and aspirations, and finding the threads that weave your unique story.

At its core, your purpose is the driving force behind your actions and decisions. It's the reason you wake up in the morning with a sense of purpose and direction. This deep-rooted motivation doesn't just fuel your ambitions; it also provides you with a profound sense of meaning and fulfillment. When you're aligned with your purpose, you're more likely to experience a sense of flow, where time seems to slip away as you engage in activities that resonate with your core essence.

However, the path to discovering your purpose is not always straightforward. It's not uncommon to be influenced by external expectations, societal norms, and the pursuit of material goals. These influences can obscure your true desires and prevent you from recognizing what truly ignites your soul.

The journey of self-discovery often begins with introspection. This involves taking the time to reflect on your passions, interests, talents, and values. Consider what activities make you lose track of time, what subjects you could talk about endlessly, and what brings you genuine joy. These clues can lead you to the heart of your purpose.

Unearthing your purpose also involves acknowledging and embracing your strengths and uniqueness. Each person possesses a set of talents, skills, and qualities that makes them distinct. Recognizing and nurturing these strengths can guide you toward roles and endeavors that allow you to shine and make a positive impact.

As you explore your passions and strengths, you'll likely start to identify patterns and themes that resonate with you. These patterns can provide insights into the direction your purpose might take. It's also valuable to seek inspiration from role models, mentors, and individuals who are already aligned with their purpose. Their stories can offer guidance and perspectives that illuminate your own path.

Importantly, the process of discovering your purpose is ongoing. It's not a one-time revelation but rather a continuous journey of growth and exploration. Your purpose might evolve as you gain new experiences, learn more about yourself, and adapt to changing circumstances.

Ultimately, embracing your purpose empowers you to live a life that's deeply authentic and meaningful. It guides your choices, motivates your actions, and infuses your days with a sense of purposeful direction. By engaging in activities that align with your purpose, you contribute to your own wellbeing while also making a positive impact on the world around you. Your purpose becomes a guiding light that illuminates your path, enriches your life, and allows you to share your unique gifts with the world.

What is Your WHY?

Understanding the importance of identifying your WHY and how it influences your pursuit of a dream future is powerful. Delving deep into your motivations allows you to establish a strong foundation for your goals. When challenges arise, and they inevitably will, having a clear and compelling WHY provides you with the strength to persevere.

In times of difficulty, it's easy to feel discouraged or tempted to give up. This is where your WHY becomes your anchor. It's the reason that you keep moving forward when obstacles seem insurmountable. It's a source of inspiration that reminds you why you started in the first place and what you're striving to achieve.

Throughout life, many of us find ourselves caught up in fulfilling other people's expectations and dreams. But when you discover your own WHY, it's a transformative experience. Suddenly, you're not just drifting along; you're guided by a purpose that's uniquely yours. This shift in perspective can bring about incredible changes.

One remarkable aspect of understanding your WHY is the way it attracts new opportunities and connections. As you align your actions with your purpose, you draw like-minded individuals into your orbit. These are the people who understand your journey, share your values, and are willing to support and guide you. It's as if the universe conspires to introduce you to the right people at the right time.

The process of self-discovery and clarifying your WHY can be a catalyst for personal growth. It encourages you to uncover your true passions and aspirations. This, in turn, attracts resources and knowledge that are relevant to your path. Suddenly, you find yourself encountering exactly what you need to move forward. It's almost as if the universe responds to your newfound clarity by providing you with the tools you require.

In the forthcoming chapter, the focus will be on how your life evolves when you embrace a full understanding of Manifestation, Gratitude, and Action. These elements combine to create a powerful equation that propels you toward remarkable results. By harnessing these principles, you tap into the potential to shape your reality and achieve what might initially seem unbelievable. The next chapter explains how my newfound wisdom impacted my life.

CHAPTER 2
CREATING A LIFE BEYOND LIMITS

Crafting a Life Without Boundaries

Following years of grappling with and facing stagnation in my pursuit of progress, I had at last attained proficiency in incorporating manifestation into my life. Armed with a constructive outlook, a sense of gratitude, and the knack for only challenging the person I was the day before, my life embarked on a journey of unparalleled growth!

Making an Impact

Through my journey in writing, I unearthed a profound passion for aiding others. This realization propelled me to establish my nonprofit organization, Driving Single Parents Inc. Its mission: To empower deserving single parents by providing them with vehicles, entirely cost-free.

It's important to remember that when I initiated this venture, I was driving a Toyota RAV4 with over 125,000 miles, purchased for $3,500 in cash. My income was average, and I had to continuously battle self-doubt. While my passion burned brightly, I questioned whether others would take me seriously, considering I was still navigating my own life challenges, let alone trying to solve transportation issues for other single parents.

Yet, the vision of the nonprofit was so vivid in my mind that it was undeniable. Within a mere 24 hours of conceptualizing the idea, I had built a website and formulated a business plan. In the subsequent weeks, we handed over the first vehicle to a deserving recipient. The first car was gifted to a single father whose life had taken a tragic turn. He had lost his wife, his vehicle, and even his right leg in a devastating accident with a drunk driver. This unfortunate incident abruptly transformed him into an unexpected single parent, facing immense challenges and responsibilities. Despite the hardships he endured, he continued to persevere in his role as a father, demonstrating remarkable strength and resilience. The gift of the car not only provided him with much-needed transportation but also symbolized a glimmer of hope and support in the midst of his difficult journey.

Since its inception in 2017, Driving Single Parents Inc. has made a positive impact on numerous single-parent families. The vehicles we've provided have served as tools to elevate these families' overall circumstances. Some have pursued higher education, secured better-paying jobs, and even achieved the dream of homeownership. The vehicles signify more than just transportation; they're a symbol of hope and progress.

The profound impact of our mission is evident in the fact that four of our beneficiaries have assumed roles as board members, contributing their personal experiences and valuable perspectives to our cause. Their active engagement substantially contributes to the accomplishment of our goal to empower single parents, allowing them to regain control over their lives.

The conception of this nonprofit was spontaneous, emerging over dinner one evening. By translating the idea into action, I paved the way for Driving Single Parents Inc. to come to life. My story underscores the truth that having all the answers is not a prerequisite. Transforming your thoughts and aspirations into action is the key to discovering their potential. Even if an idea doesn't pan out, failure is an opportunity for growth. Thomas Edison's words ring true: "I didn't fail, I just found 10,000 ways that didn't work." The key is to keep going, driven by your clear vision. Taking that step matters, and things often fall into place in surprising ways.

Personal, Professional, and Relationship Transformation

Before I took charge of my emotional wellbeing and learned the art of manifestation, I was consistently entangled in unhealthy relationships. A recurring pattern in my adult life was being a "fixer"—someone who saw the warning signs and issues but chose to ignore them, hoping I could mend the problems and salvage the relationship. This pattern persisted in all my past relationships. I would shoulder the weight of the other person's shortcomings, pouring in extra effort to mend them and mold them to fit my life.

It wasn't until I embarked on a journey of self-discovery that I confronted this significant hurdle and uncovered its root cause. This realization prompted a profound shift in my perspective on friendships and relationships. I abandoned the practice of ignoring red flags and began upholding my standards. I consciously allowed individuals into my life who uplifted me. This shift was transformative. Within months, I encountered my best friend, who eventually became my husband and blessed me with two fantastic bonus children. He treats me, along with my daughters, with the kindness and respect we deserve.

With positivity, love, and stability taking root, my life underwent a remarkable evolution. A new work opportunity materialized, placing me in an entirely different setting where growth and prospects were abundant. Bolstered by newfound self-assurance and belief, my career surged forward. I embraced fresh opportunities and saw my professional trajectory soar to heights I hadn't deemed possible.

Reflecting on the past 15 years, it's evident that multiple career advancements had come my way, only for me to decline them due to a lack of confidence and self-imposed limitations. Yet, as I mastered the principles of manifestation and self-empowerment, I overcame these barriers and embraced the avenues of growth that had long been within reach. The transformation was not only in my career but also in my personal life and relationships.

The key takeaway is that personal growth in emotional wellbeing and the willingness to manifest can catalyze an incredible transformation across all spheres of life. By acknowledging and addressing our own limitations, we can unlock opportunities that were once obscured by self-doubt. This journey is a testament to the extraordinary power of self-discovery and conscious change.

Conquering Self-Doubt

Despite the array of accomplishments I had achieved, one looming fear remained to be conquered. Throughout my life, I had perceived myself as an outsider, harboring a relentlessly self-critical mindset. The idea of drawing attention to myself filled me with dread, stemming from a deep-seated fear of ridicule. In my early years, I would meticulously rehearse paragraphs before speaking aloud and obsessively analyze a single question before daring to voice it.

Upon establishing Driving Single Parents, a significant aspect of my role involved giving interviews and raising awareness about our impactful work. However, my persistent apprehension and fear of public speaking held me back. Recognizing the need to break free from this hindrance, I resolved to overcome this seemingly irrational fear. I added this aspiration to my vision board and commenced writing about confidently speaking on podcasts, public platforms, and interviews, casting aside fear and self-doubt.

In due course, I began to respond affirmatively to every interview request, even though the prospect of public speaking left me trembling. This marked the beginning of my journey to dismantle self-doubt. With relentless practice and an ever-increasing number of interviews, I mustered the courage to confront my fear head-on. Gradually, the fear receded as I found myself becoming more proficient in the art of public speaking.

The transformation was a result of consistent effort and determination to defy my own insecurities. While the fear didn't vanish entirely, I had learned to navigate it with grace and resilience. This journey serves as a testament to the potency of visualization, persistence, and pushing through discomfort. Overcoming self-doubt requires acknowledging its presence and committing to challenging it, step by step.

Exceeding My Own Expectations

Becoming an author was a notion that initially seemed far from attainable for me. The idea of writing a book appeared so absurd that I dismissed it outright when it first crossed my mind. I convinced myself it was an unattainable feat, assuming I lacked the intelligence and would inevitably face negative judgments from those close to me. I believed my role as a struggling single mother confined me to flying under the radar, focusing on day-to-day survival and creating a better life for my daughters. The idea of becoming a published author was unequivocally on my "impossible" list.

Fast forward about five years, and I found myself co-authoring my first book, *Shattering the Stigma of Single Motherhood*, stepping into the realm of published authors. Looking back, I realized I could have achieved this much earlier had I only embraced self-belief, documented my aspirations, and translated my thoughts into action. This story mirrors the experiences of many individuals who sideline their dreams, deeming them unrealistic or fearing external judgment, ultimately abandoning them before encountering failure. I, too, followed this pattern for much of my life.

It wasn't until I decided to shed concern for others' opinions, practice gratitude for what I had, believe in my capabilities, and solely compete with my past self that my life began to transform. This shift in mindset allowed my life to take form in unexpected ways. I hadn't realized the extent to which I had been limiting my own potential.

The takeaway from my journey is that we often underestimate our abilities and allow external opinions to hinder our progress. Embracing self-belief, gratitude, and a growth-oriented mindset can be immensely empowering. Disregarding external judgment and focusing on personal growth and progress enables us to surpass our own expectations and truly live up to our potential. My experience is a reminder that we are often the main obstacle standing in our own way, and overcoming this hurdle can lead to profound transformation.

Embrace Fear and Take Action

I embraced my fear and co-authored that book, which eventually led to me becoming an Amazon International Best-Selling Author. The sense of accomplishment was overwhelming, considering how I pushed through my fear. I couldn't help but reflect on how I could have easily stayed in my comfort zone, allowing that opportunity to pass me by. But this time, I seized the moment. I did it, and I felt genuine pride in my achievement. The experience opened up a world of incredible people, a supportive community that valued collaboration over competition, and an unwavering support system. The blend of pride, joy, and accomplishment without any regret is etched into my memory.

Following the success of *Shattering the Stigma of Single Motherhood,* I was presented with opportunities to co-author multiple books. However, none resonated with me until I heard the title of a forthcoming book set to be released in the spring of 2023. At that moment, I knew I had found my next book project.

So, I accepted the invitation to co-author the anthology *Overcoming Self-Sabotage.* When I say my passion lies in helping others, it's an understatement. With the nonprofit and the release of the two books I co-authored, I confronted my fear head-on, knowing that my own story, particularly the challenging parts, could resonate with and assist others. Sharing my struggles has illuminated a path for many to recognize that their past doesn't dictate their identity. Regardless of origins in poverty, experiences of domestic violence, single parenthood, or growing up in a single-parent household, we all have aspects of our lives that weren't ideal. What truly matters is how we transform those experiences into purpose.

Realizing this, I've come to understand that our past doesn't define us. We all hold the power to decide where our stories lead. The choices we make either propel us into the potential of our purpose or hold us back. This choice is entirely ours. The power to shatter self-limiting beliefs and propel ourselves to the next level resides within us. Recognizing this truth and acting on it is the key to achieving our loftiest aspirations.

Entrepreneurial Journey

While co-authoring *Overcoming Self-Sabotage*, I embarked on yet another significant venture—establishing my own business, CF Views LLC. This venture sprang from my profound yearning to make a positive impact on others. My business encompasses various realms, from offering advertising space to providing coaching services in Nonprofit Startup, Life, and Confidence areas. It also includes the sale of the books I've authored.

Being a business owner and CEO is a realization of a dream I had held close. CF Views LLC serves as the parent company for all my projects. Once again, the power of writing played a pivotal role in materializing this business. Writing helped me harness the principles of manifestation, converting aspirations into tangible reality.

The most incredible aspect of this journey is that every step doesn't feel like work at all. Each facet of my endeavors resonates deeply with me, and I find enjoyment in every element of what I do. The alignment between my passions and my business activities has turned my work into something fulfilling and purpose-driven. This fusion of ambition, action, and fulfillment underscores the power of turning one's desires into tangible ventures. Through CF Views LLC, I've not only transformed my aspirations into reality but have also created a platform to extend meaningful assistance to others.

Elevating to New Heights

I had the privilege of publishing both my books through an incredible publishing company, She Rises Studios, owned by an inspiring mother-daughter team dedicated to empowering women worldwide. In late 2022, I learned about their newest endeavor, *Fenix TV*. Over the following months, the idea of hosting my own TV show was presented to me. Yet again, my instinctive response was a resounding no. Public speaking fears still lingered, and the thought of hosting a show with no experience seemed preposterous. However, in January 2023, a spark ignited within me. A voice in my head whispered, "What if?"

So, I started to write. Could I truly become a TV show host? Was this something I'd even want to do? Questions flooded my mind. Through persistent journaling, the answers emerged. The concept crystallized—having a show focused on aiding people could be immensely fulfilling.

This marked the birth of *Little Give with Cindy*, a TV show on Fenix TV, broadcasted to over 100 countries every Sunday. The show revolves around highlighting ordinary individuals accomplishing extraordinary feats to help others. Upon establishing Driving Single Parents, many people inquired about what distinguished me and led me to conceive the nonprofit organization. My response? I'm just an ordinary person who recognized a need and found a way to address it. Starting a grassroots nonprofit is no small feat, and raising awareness is a major challenge. Thus, *Little Give* was conceived to showcase regular people who decided to take action, thereby impacting others.

Through hosting the show, I've connected with profoundly inspirational individuals globally. Every interview reaffirms my decision to embrace this opportunity. I've absorbed knowledge from guests tirelessly working to improve the world. Through *Little Give*, I encourage others to give a little more every day. It's not about grand gestures; it's about embracing the impact of every "Little Give." Guests share an example of a small act each of us can do in our community. They also recount a time when someone's seemingly minor gesture had a lasting impact on their lives.

Indeed, these two questions serve as powerful reminders of the impact that small gestures can have on others. By sharing personal experiences and reflecting on the ways in which seemingly minor actions have left a significant imprint, individuals are encouraged to recognize the ripple effect of kindness. These questions help magnify the significance of everyday acts and highlight the ways in which they can lead to positive change and a chain reaction of goodwill in the world.

The show's far-reaching influence has resulted in the creation of a podcast spin-off called *Little Give—Podcast*, which can be easily accessed on popular streaming platforms. This extension of the original show has taken the essence of *Little Give* to an even broader audience, allowing listeners from various corners of the world to engage with its meaningful content. Through this podcast, the impactful messages and heartwarming stories that define *Little Give* are now available in an audio format that offers convenience and accessibility to those seeking inspiration, kindness, and positive perspectives.

Through sharing my personal journey of challenges and triumphs, I hope to underscore the profound impact that manifestation can have on one's life. The transformation from battling insecurities and self-imposed limitations to becoming the person I am today serves as a testament to the potential of taking charge of your own destiny. The first step is to break free from procrastination and uncertainties, and instead, clarify your aspirations. Put pen to paper, outline your dreams, and meticulously plan the path forward. Progress may be gradual, but each day's stride, no matter how small, takes you closer to your objective. Always remember the words of Bob Proctor: "If you can see it in your mind, you can hold it in your hand."

Harnessing the power of manifestation, a strong sense of purpose, unwavering determination, consistent action, and genuine gratitude propelled me to the forefront of accomplishments. From being the Founder/CEO of Driving Single Parents Inc., an Amazon International Best-Selling Author, Business Owner, Nonprofit and Confidence Coach, Entrepreneur, Speaker, and Podcaster, to hosting the *Little Give* TV Show, I've been able to shape a multifaceted and fulfilling life. My journey, starting from humble beginnings, serves as a testament that if I can achieve this transformation, so can you. Manifestation is a catalyst for change, and in the next chapter, I'll provide you with guidance on integrating these principles into your life, embarking on a path toward abundance and self-discovery.

CHAPTER 3
TIPS, TRICKS, & TRUTHS

A Foundation to Begin

The starting point to your journey is embracing each day with gratitude. This wasn't always easy for me, especially when I began practicing manifestation. I was so focused on what I lacked, rather than appreciating what I already possessed. When I started waking up every morning and acknowledging what I was grateful for, my perspective shifted significantly.

I initiated this by cultivating thoughts of gratitude, even for the smallest things, right before getting out of bed. Then, I devoted three minutes to writing in my gratitude journal. This marked the pivotal moment in my personal path toward abundance. It's a foundational step that allowed me to recognize the wealth of blessings already present in my life.

Eliminate Negativity

Spreading negativity serves no purpose. Dwelling on unpleasant situations won't alter them; it will only nurture more negativity.

Thinking or vocalizing negative thoughts fuels a cycle that leads to increased negativity, frustration, and anger, with no productive outcome.

While you can't dictate others' actions, you can control your own reactions and behaviors. A valuable guideline is to abstain from voicing thoughts that don't contribute positively to you or others. A principle my grandmother taught me: "If you don't have something nice to say, don't say anything at all." This sage advice reminds us to choose our words wisely and opt for positivity instead of contributing to a cycle of negativity.

Abandon Judgment

In our intricate world, each person carries experiences, struggles, and triumphs that often remain hidden from the external eye. While we may interact with others, it's important to remember that we don't have access to the full scope of their lives and emotions. This realization serves as a crucial reminder to abstain from judgment, as appearances can be deceiving.

When we judge or critique others, we risk overlooking the complexity of their journey. Our perceptions can be clouded by our own biases, insecurities, and limited understanding. As the saying goes, "Don't judge a book by its cover." The same applies to people.

By choosing to withhold judgement, we foster a culture of empathy and understanding. This not only benefits others but also has a profound impact on our own wellbeing. Letting go of the impulse to criticize or compare ourselves to others alleviates the unnecessary burden of negativity. The mental space once occupied by judgment becomes available for more productive and fulfilling thoughts.

In essence, breaking free from the habit of judgment allows us to see the beauty in diversity and the richness of each individual's unique story. It reminds us that everyone is fighting their own battles and striving for their own versions of success. Embracing compassion and refraining from judgment leads to a more harmonious and positive existence, both for ourselves and those around us.

Give Grace

As previously highlighted, we seldom grasp the full extent of someone else's day. We've all encountered instances of road rage from fellow drivers or experienced encounters with irritable employees at checkout counters. It's imperative to grant these individuals grace, recognizing that their frustration likely stems from circumstances unrelated to your interaction.

Rest assured, the source of their agitation is unlikely to be you. There's likely an external factor causing stress and anger. Instead of letting the negativity spread, choose to remain understanding. Don't dwell on the negative encounter, and avoid discussing it with others. Refrain from amplifying negativity and always give others the benefit of the doubt.

Remember, your reaction is the sole aspect you can control. By responding without negativity, you cultivate a more positive atmosphere for all involved. Demonstrating empathy and choosing to be gracious creates a ripple effect that contributes to a more harmonious environment.

Pro Tip: Transform Your Mindset

Allowing negative thoughts to occupy your mind only fuels a cycle of negativity. The emotions these thoughts evoke aren't beneficial for you or anyone around you. Remember, if a thought pattern doesn't contribute positively, you possess the power to switch your mental channel. Direct your emotions toward a happier and more constructive way of thinking. By taking charge of your mindset, you shape a more fulfilling and productive path for yourself.

Shifting Your Mindset: A Guide

The concept of mindset is pervasive, but effecting a true shift requires conscious effort. It's not a simple task, and it demands dedicated practice. So, how do you genuinely transform your mindset? Let me explain: The most potent method involves training your brain to perceive the positive aspects of life. This necessitates actively steering away from negative thoughts and emotions.

At the outset, this process will require manual intervention; it won't come easily. Yet, as you consistently adopt the habit of cultivating positive thoughts, regardless of circumstances, you'll find yourself gaining control over your emotions and reactions. It's a practice that can be challenging but immensely rewarding.

As your mindset evolves, you'll observe changes in the way others communicate with you and the way you're treated. Suddenly, you'll recognize that people are generally kind and generous. The shift is profound: Where once you were fixated on negativity, your mind will now naturally gravitate toward positivity. This newly cultivated positive mindset will reveal the good in situations that previously went unnoticed. In time, the positive aspects of life will present themselves more frequently, shaping a more uplifting and harmonious existence.

Pro Tip: Break the Negative Cycle

When embarking on the journey of transforming negative thoughts into positive ones, consider this effective technique that aided me greatly. In the beginning, I employed a simple rubber band placed around my wrist. Each time a negative thought surfaced, I'd give the rubber band a SNAP. This method served as a sharp reminder, helping me track and address my thoughts effectively.

Negative thoughts can sometimes slip in unnoticed and multiply. The rubber band method swiftly held me accountable for my thoughts, eventually training my mind to veer away from negativity. This technique might seem somewhat dramatic, and it may not suit everyone. However, for me, it played a crucial role in rapidly reorienting my thought patterns.

Remember, the goal is to be mindful of your thoughts and replace negative ones with positive alternatives. Whether it's the rubber band method or another strategy, the objective remains the same: to train your brain to cultivate positivity and actively guide your mindset toward a more constructive and fulfilling outlook.

Eliminating Self-Doubt

Self-doubt and self-sabotage were powerful obstacles that hindered my progress across various facets of life. Growing up surrounded by scarcity, I battled feelings of unworthiness and an incessant belief that something was fundamentally flawed within me. This shattered my confidence and deterred me from daring to dream or pursuing any ambitions.

Conquering self-sabotage requires acknowledging your intrinsic worth and fostering an unshakable belief in your distinct skill set. Recognize that you possess a unique collection of abilities, setting you apart from others. You are deserving, and your potential is boundless; you can achieve whatever you set your mind to.

Once you shift your perspective to one of unwavering belief in yourself, you'll experience a remarkable transformation in your self-perception. This newfound sense of self-assurance will radiate in every aspect of your life. Remember the words of Warren Buffett: "The most important investment you can make is in yourself." By investing in your self-belief and dispelling self-doubt, you lay the foundation for unprecedented personal growth and success.

Pro Tip: Tune in to Your Self-Talk

When challenges emerge, a valuable practice is to attentively listen to your own reactions. Pay close attention to the words you employ, especially when negativity creeps in. Observe instances where you use phrases like "I can't," "I won't," "but," "I could if," and "when."

This heightened self-awareness serves as the initial step towards authentic manifestation. Rewiring your thought patterns and training your brain requires meticulous attention to the language you use. By consciously reshaping your self-talk, you lay the groundwork for transforming your beliefs and ultimately paving the way to manifesting your aspirations.

Incorporate and apply the following steps as a helpful guide during your journey of manifestation. By integrating these principles into your approach, you can navigate the path toward manifesting your desires with greater clarity and purpose.

Step 1: Start Writing

The act of writing serves as a foundational step in your journey to abundance. It's a process that begins to set your intentions in motion. Don't be discouraged if your initial writing feels disjointed or unclear. The goal is to start the flow of thoughts, even if they appear fragmented at first. Commit to spending at least 6 minutes each day to write down your aspirations. This could involve scribbling down any words, phrases, or ideas that come to mind. Over time, as you consistently engage in this practice, you'll notice your thoughts evolving, connecting, and forming a coherent plan. You might find it beneficial to split this practice into three-minute sessions in the morning and before bedtime, creating bookends for your day's reflections.

Step 2: Find Your Why

Delve deeper into your goals by uncovering your "why." This intrinsic motivation serves as a powerful driving force. When challenges arise—as they inevitably will—your "why" becomes the anchor that keeps you steadfast. If your dreams have a meaningful impact beyond yourself, such as benefiting your loved ones or your community, you'll discover a renewed determination to persevere. The "why" becomes your unwavering commitment, helping you navigate through setbacks and obstacles with resolve.

Step 3: Visualize Your Goals

Visualization is a potent tool in the manifestation process. Begin to imagine your goals as vividly as possible. If you're aiming to establish a new business, visualize its name, its purpose, and its impact. Allow yourself to see the details unfolding in your mind's eye. Take these mental images and put them onto paper. Sketch out the beginnings of a business plan or jot down the essential components of your vision. Even if it feels rough or incomplete, the act of visualizing and writing anchors your aspirations in reality, guiding your thoughts toward concrete plans of action.

Pro Tip: Read and Learn

One of the most effective ways to accelerate your journey to abundance is through learning. Just like a GPS guiding you with optimal routes and shortcuts, books and resources offer insights and wisdom that others have gleaned from their experiences. By reading, listening to audiobooks, or engaging in learning materials relevant to your goals, you're tapping into a wealth of knowledge that can propel you forward faster and more efficiently.

Step 4: Surround Yourself with Like-Minded People

Building a supportive network is essential. Seek out individuals who share your ambitions or who have already achieved similar goals. Engaging with like-minded people can provide invaluable guidance, motivation, and a sense of belonging. Online communities, forums, and local groups can offer opportunities to connect with individuals who understand your journey and can provide perspectives and insights that inspire and uplift.

Step 5: Dream Big with Vision Boards

The power of visualization can be further enhanced by creating a vision board. This visual representation allows you to translate your dreams and goals into tangible images and words. Your vision board becomes a dynamic tool that reinforces your aspirations every time you see it. But remember, a vision board is not just about aesthetics—it's about selecting images, quotes, and elements that deeply resonate with your desired accomplishments. As you create your board, immerse yourself in the emotions that arise from achieving those goals.

Pro Tip: Visualize and Feel It

A vision board is not a mere collection of images; it's an embodiment of your future achievements. Engage with your vision board daily, not only to see it, but also to feel the emotions associated with accomplishing your goals. By vividly imagining and experiencing feelings of success, you're reinforcing the positive energy needed to manifest your dreams.

By following this step-by-step guide, you're actively shifting your mindset, cultivating positivity, and taking actionable steps toward a life of abundance. Each step builds upon the previous one, creating a comprehensive approach that empowers you to manifest your dreams and create a future filled with fulfillment and success.

Step 6: Cultivate Positive Feelings

Imagine the elation you'll experience when you've realized your dreams—the exhilaration of starting your own business, the sense of accomplishment that accompanies buying your dream car, or the joy of moving into the home you've always envisioned. These emotions aren't just fleeting; they become the fuel that propels you forward. By immersing yourself in these positive feelings, you create a strong emotional connection to your goals. This connection motivates you to push through challenges and setbacks, as you constantly remind yourself of the incredible emotions waiting for you on the other side of success.

Step 7: Embrace Consistency

Think of your dreams as seeds planted in the fertile soil of your mind. Like a farmer, you must consistently nurture and tend to these seeds. Just as plants need water, sunlight, and care to grow, your dreams require your unwavering attention and effort. The act of consistently revisiting your goals, reviewing your progress, and refining your plans keeps your intentions alive and thriving. While it's natural to seek immediate results, remember that growth takes time. Trust the process, stay committed, and maintain a consistent rhythm of action to witness the gradual transformation of your dreams into reality.

Step 8: Control Your Thoughts

Harness the incredible power of your thoughts by consciously choosing positivity. The more you focus on positive thoughts, the more you invite positive experiences into your life. When you find negative thoughts creeping in, take charge of your mental landscape. Redirect your mind to thoughts of gratitude, possibility, and success. This practice of mental discipline rewires your brain over time, making positivity your default setting. As you align your thoughts with your desired outcomes, you create a magnetic force that attracts opportunities, people, and circumstances that resonate with your aspirations.

Step 9: Respond, Don't React

In a world filled with varying perspectives and behaviors, it's important to choose a mindful response over a knee-jerk reaction. When faced with someone else's actions that trigger negativity or frustration, pause before responding. Consider the possibility that their behavior may be influenced by factors outside of your awareness. Respond with empathy, understanding, and kindness, regardless of external circumstances. This approach not only preserves your inner peace but also prevents unnecessary conflicts that can hinder your journey toward abundance.

Step 10: Curate Your Inner Circle

Your environment shapes your mindset and influences your outcomes. Evaluate the people you interact with regularly—your inner circle.

Surround yourself with individuals who share your positive outlook, support your aspirations, and encourage your growth. While you can't always choose your family or colleagues, you can choose how much influence they have on your thoughts and emotions. Prioritize spending time with those who inspire, uplift, and challenge you to reach new heights. As you cultivate relationships that align with your goals, you create a fertile ground for your dreams to flourish.

By embracing these expanded steps, you're embarking on a comprehensive journey toward manifesting abundance. This journey involves aligning your thoughts, emotions, and actions with your goals. As you stay consistent, maintain positivity, and curate your surroundings, you're creating a powerful momentum that propels you toward your desired future. With each step, you're not just inching closer to your dreams—you're actively designing a life that reflects your true potential and abundance.

"Lifting as We Climb" –Mary Church Terrell

This is a quote that truly resonates with me. It's something I've always felt drawn to, a natural inclination to lend a helping hand and share my journey in the hope that it might uplift others. Helping people navigate their challenges and find solutions has always been part of who I am. There's a unique sense of accomplishment in guiding others toward a life full of possibilities.

This book is my way of explaining how manifesting truly works. We all possess the incredible ability to achieve greatness in our lives. By following the steps I've laid out, you'd be surprised at how much your life can shift. And even if nothing else comes from it, you'll undoubtedly find yourself feeling more positive about everything you already have.

Through my personal journey and the insights I've shared, I've aimed to light the way to abundance. These steps aren't just about practical actions; they're about shaping your mindset and nurturing your spirit for success. By embracing gratitude, positivity, and unwavering self-belief, you can turn your dreams into tangible reality.

I've witnessed firsthand how dedicating myself to growth and empowerment can lead to a life of opportunities. Manifesting isn't some unreachable concept—it's a practical approach that can be cultivated. By following these steps, you too can bring your aspirations to life.

In the spirit of "lifting as we climb," I hope my experiences and advice encourage you to embark on your transformative journeys. Armed with these tools and a newfound mindset, you can manifest your desires and create a life with purpose and fulfillment.

Bonus Story:

As I delved into the practice of manifesting, I found that updating my vision board every three months was a powerful way to keep my goals and desires at the forefront of my mind. In March of 2023, I decided to target my fitness routine for the upcoming quarter. While I had always enjoyed the rhythm of walking and running, I felt the pull to challenge myself further and engage in something more intense. Even though my schedule was packed, I took the leap and added this new fitness goal to my vision board. Little did I know that this seemingly simple action would set off a chain of events that perfectly exemplified the power of manifesting.

On June 10th, I had the honor of interviewing Krystalore Crews, the inspiring owner of Crews Beyond Limits, as a guest on my TV show, *Little Give with Cindy*. During our enlightening conversation, Krystalore shared her remarkable story and introduced me to her fitness program. As I listened, I felt a strong connection to her journey and was genuinely captivated by the philosophy and methodology behind

Crews Beyond Limits. It didn't take long for me to decide to give the program a try, intrigued by the idea of carving out just 34 minutes a day for my wellbeing. This routine involved 30 minutes of invigorating movement, followed by four minutes of reflection and gratitude—a combination that resonated deeply with me.

However, there was a twist waiting for me just around the corner. In July 2023, about a month into my dedication to Crews Beyond Limits, my husband playfully pointed out a curious connection. He realized that the title of Chapter 2 of this book, *Creating a Life Beyond Limits*, mirrored the slogan of the very fitness program I had recently embraced—"Crews Beyond Limits." Initially, I brushed it off as a mere coincidence, but as I revisited my book trailer and took another look at my vision board, the truth became undeniable. My three-month fitness goal had materialized in an unexpected and delightful manner.

This serendipitous alignment was not random; it was a manifestation in action. The fusion of my fitness journey and the concept of manifesting had seamlessly intertwined, bringing me a real-world example of how the universe responds to focused intention. This experience reinforced the significance of each item on my vision board and how its energy can translate into tangible outcomes. Here's a breakdown of how my manifestations on the vision board aligned with my newfound fitness journey:

1. *Wake up early!* The fitness videos were broadcast live at the early hour of 5:00 a.m. or 5:30 a.m. CST three days a week. This aligned perfectly with my vision board's aspiration to wake up early, urging me to embrace this practice to engage in the program.

2. *Meet the right people at the right time!* Connecting with Krystalore Crews and exploring Crews Beyond Limits happened at precisely the right time according to my vision

board's timeline for conquering my fitness goal. It was a testament to the universe's ability to guide me to the right opportunities because I was aligned with my intentions.

3. *Yes, You Can* Throughout the workouts, Krystalore's encouraging phrase, "Yes, You Can," resonated with me. Interestingly, the affirmation aligned with what I had on my vision board, showing how my thoughts and actions were connected.

Testing my Vision Board

Another instance where my vision board proved its worth was in March 2022 when I boldly added an image of a Tesla to my vision board. Honestly, I had my doubts about this one. I couldn't fathom how this seemingly expensive car would fit into my life. But, as fate would have it, the universe conspired in unexpected ways. By November 2022, I was behind the wheel of my Tesla, an acquisition that not only fulfilled my desire but also made financial sense beyond my wildest imagination.

This experience was a reminder that the practice of manifesting isn't just about wishful thinking; it's about aligning our thoughts, intentions, and actions to create meaningful change. It showed me that manifesting doesn't always follow a linear path and that sometimes the universe works in beautifully unexpected ways to fulfill our desires. The bonus story of my fitness journey illustrates the magic that happens when we set clear intentions, trust the process, and remain open to the unique ways our goals can come to fruition. These two stories are just a glimpse of how the power of manifesting has woven its magic into my life, showing me that even the most seemingly improbable desires can become a reality.

Reflecting on these stories, there's a clear thread that runs through both: the importance of taking action. You see, it's not enough to visualize, wish, or hope for something to materialize. It's the intentional steps we take—inspired, guided, and nudged by our vision—that bridge the gap between imagination and reality. When I set out to experience the transformative Crews Beyond Limits fitness program, I embraced action and it turned out to be a perfect fit. Similarly, my desire to own a Tesla found its realization not just in the images on my vision board, but in the practical steps I took to explore, research, and uncover the hidden opportunities that made it a feasible goal.

These stories highlight a crucial insight: our preconceived notions of limitations can often mislead us. We're prone to assuming that certain things are beyond our grasp without truly investigating the potential avenues that lie before us. The key, as I've learned, is to challenge those assumptions, to investigate, and to act. For instance, the affordability of a Tesla with its absence of fuel expenses, unexpected rebates, and lower insurance costs shattered the illusion that owning a Tesla was out of reach.

(Please refer to the attached images of my personal vision board that illustrate the concepts mentioned above.)

It's important to acknowledge that a life built on manifesting isn't exempt from life's ups and downs. I face my share of challenges, experience tough days, and grapple with negative thoughts just like anyone else. The difference lies in my approach. When faced with adversity, I see it as an opportunity to learn, to evolve, and to continue striving for the next goal. The reality is that this journey isn't always smooth sailing; it's a continual process of growth and development. And that's okay—because these setbacks only serve to enrich the story of my journey.

So, as you embark on your own path to manifesting a life beyond limits, remember that it's not about perfection or immunity to challenges. It's about persistence, determination, and a willingness to push forward even when the going gets tough. Just as Krystalore Crews reminds us, "The Work Works, when you do the Work." The effort you invest, the actions you take, and the mindset you cultivate will shape the life you're creating. Stick with it, don't be disheartened by setbacks, and eventually, you'll look back and appreciate the strides you've made. And in those moments, you'll realize that the transformation is a testament to your dedication and the boundless potential that lies within you.

IN CONCLUSION

The journey to manifesting a life beyond limits is a powerful and transformative one. By following the steps outlined in this guide, you can tap into your inner potential and create a reality that aligns with your dreams and desires. Remember that the process starts with writing down your hopes and dreams, setting clear goals, and finding your "why" to stay motivated.

Visualization and surrounding yourself with like-minded individuals can amplify your efforts, while consistent action and a positive mindset are essential to bringing your dreams to life. Embracing gratitude, removing negativity, and letting go of self-doubt will propel you forward. Remember, you are the creator of your reality, and the power of your thoughts and actions is immense.

Through real-life stories and experiences, we've seen how these principles can work wonders in transforming lives. The journey may have its challenges, but by remaining persistent, adaptable, and open to learning, you can overcome obstacles and continue on the path of growth and abundance.

Thank you for joining me on this journey of self-discovery and empowerment. Remember, you have the power within you to manifest a life beyond limits. Keep believing in yourself, taking action, and nurturing a positive mindset. Your dreams are waiting to be realized—go out there and make them a reality!

If you're interested in learning more about my endeavors or connecting, please feel free to visit the following websites or reach out via email:

Contact:

- Email: If you have any questions or would like to connect, you can reach out to me directly at Cindy@LittleGive.com.

Websites:

- Nonprofit: If you're interested in learning more about our nonprofit organization and its mission to support single parents, you can visit DrivingSingleParents.org (https://www.drivingsingleparents.org/)

- Little Give TV Show: To learn more about the *Little Give* TV Show and its aim to highlight inspiring stories of ordinary people making extraordinary contributions, check out LittleGive.com(https://www.littlegive.com/)

- Little Give Podcast: If you prefer podcasts, you can listen to the *Little Give* podcast on major streaming platforms or directly on LittleGive.com(https://www.littlegive.com/)

- Life & Confidence Coaching, Nonprofit Startup, Books: For information about life and confidence coaching, nonprofit startup guidance, and books authored by me, please visit CFViews.com(https://www.cfviews.com/)

Fitness Program:

Crews Beyond Limits: If you're curious about the fitness program that had a positive impact on my life, you can learn more about it at KrystaloreCrews.com(https://www.krystalorecrews.com/) or reach out to Krystalore@thecrewscoach.com. Please note that I'm recommending this program based on my personal experience and genuine appreciation for its effectiveness.

Recommended Books:

If you're looking for insightful reads to expand your knowledge and perspective, consider these highly recommended books:

- *The Power of One More* by Ed Mylett
- *Think and Grow Rich* by Napoleon Hill
- *Into the Magic Shop* by James R. Doty
- *The Secret* by Rhonda Byrne
- *The 5 Second Rule* by Mel Robbins
- *Shattering the Stigma of Single Motherhood* by Jillion Zambon (Chapter 5 by Cindy Witteman)- *Overcoming Self-Sabotage* by Hanna Olivas & Adriana Luna (Chapter 3 by Cindy Witteman)

Exploring these resources can greatly contribute to your personal growth journey. Remember, knowledge without action is just potential. Applying what you've learned and taking consistent steps forward will make all the difference in manifesting the life you desire. Best of luck on your journey to a life beyond limits!

With Love
Cindy Witteman

CINDY WITTEMAN'S VISION BOARD

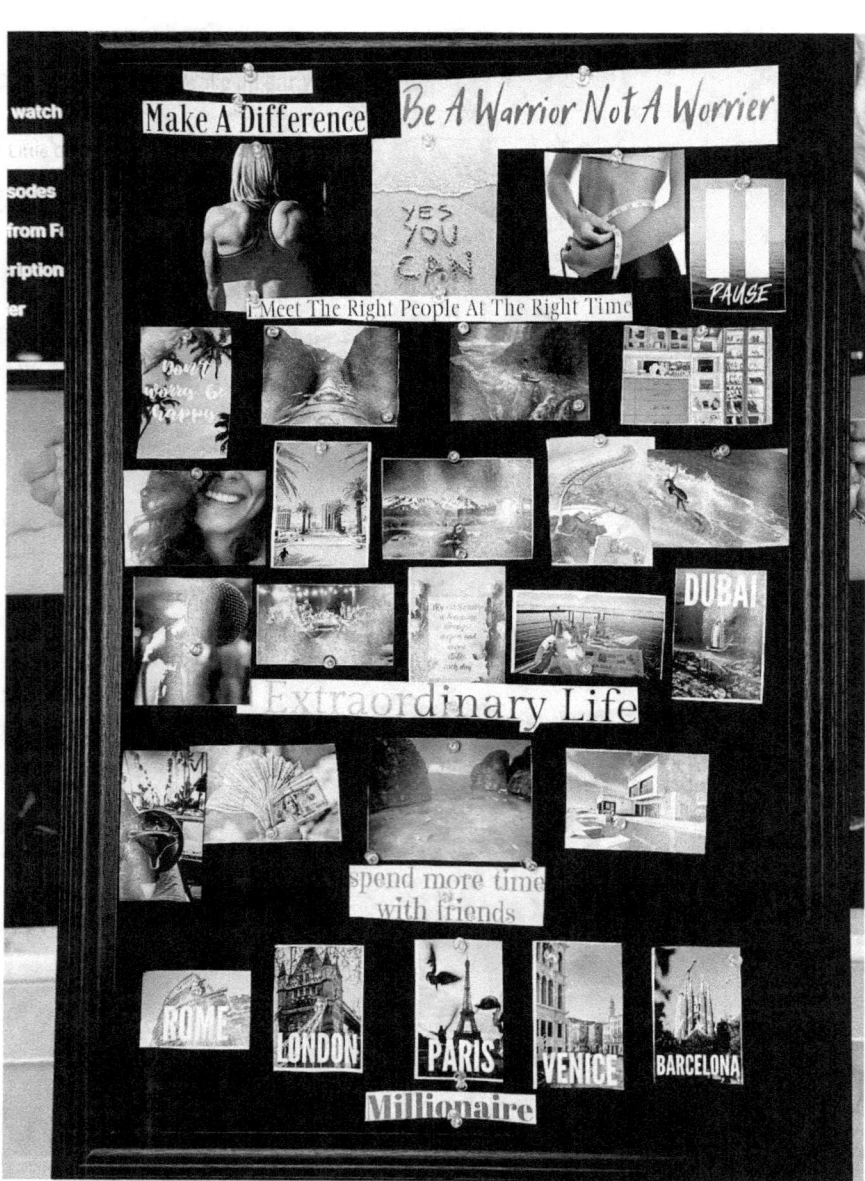

Inspirational quotes chosen by Cindy Witteman

When writing the
story of your life.
don't let anyone else
hold the pen.

THE INSPIRING
SOULS

Don't let anyone
rent a space in your
head unless they're
a good tenant.

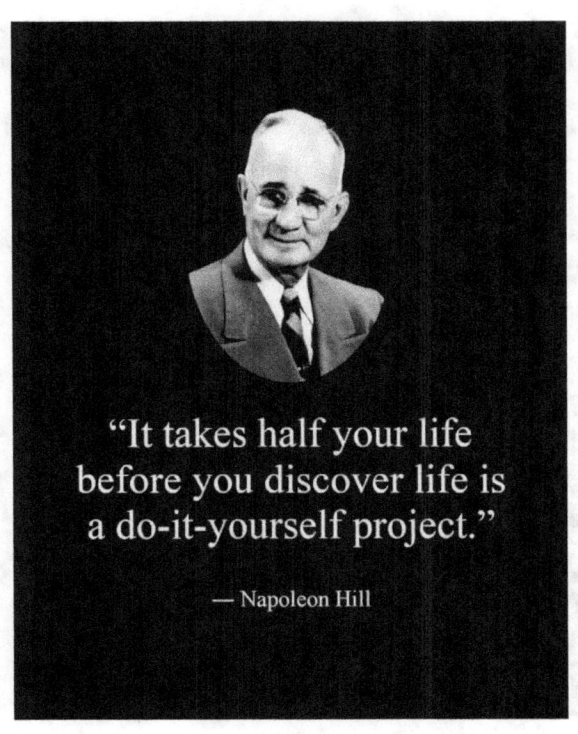

"It takes half your life before you discover life is a do-it-yourself project."

— Napoleon Hill

When you start taking care of yourself you start feeling better, you start looking better, and you start to attract better. It all starts with you.

Power of Positivity

SUCCESS

STEP 8
STEP 7
STEP 6
STEP 5
STEP 4
STEP 3
STEP 2
STEP 1

MQAQ

REMEMBER THE FIRST STEP IS ALWAYS DIFFICULT.

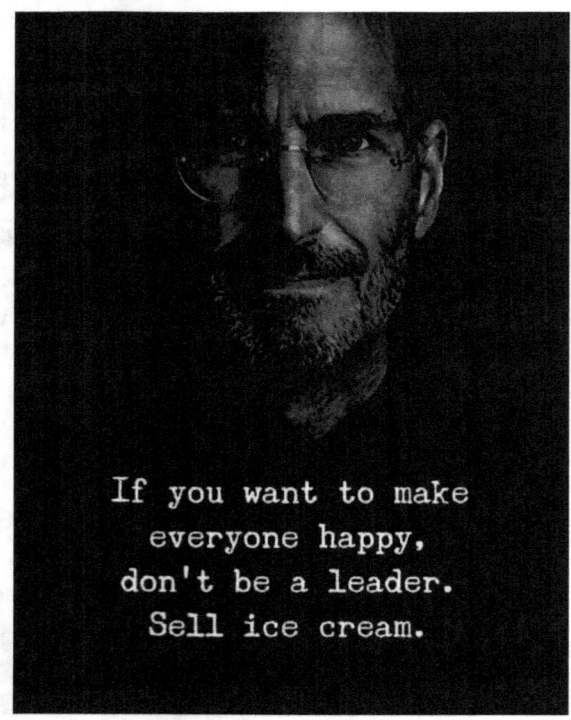

If you want to make everyone happy, don't be a leader. Sell ice cream.

DON'T let your ICE CREAM melt while you're COUNTING somebody else's SPRINKLES.

AKILAH HUGHES

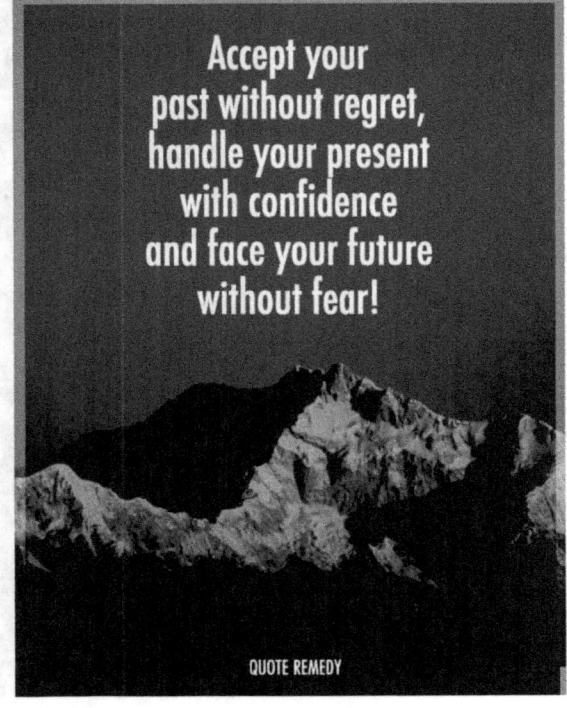

Accept your past without regret, handle your present with confidence and face your future without fear!

QUOTE REMEDY

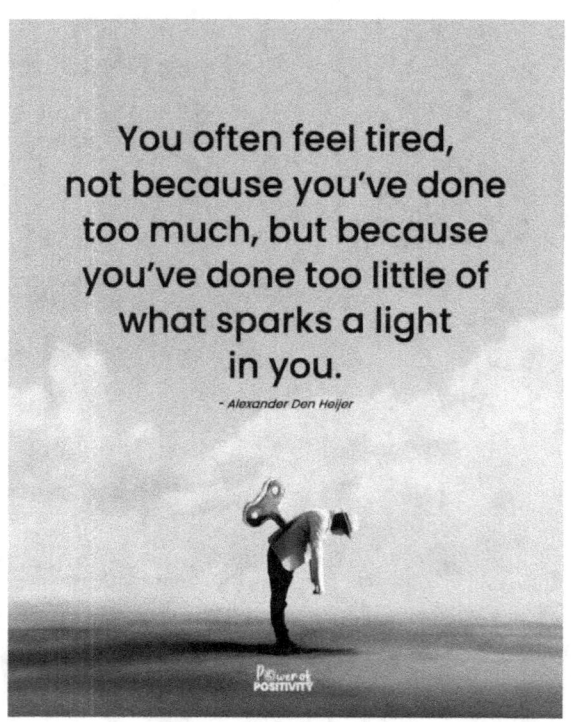

You often feel tired,
not because you've done
too much, but because
you've done too little of
what sparks a light
in you.

- Alexander Den Heijer

Power of
POSITIVITY

Life Lessons

Just a reminder in case your mind
is playing tricks on you today.

You matter. You're important.
You're loved. And your presence
on this earth makes a difference,
whether you see it or not.

June 11, 2023

Your hardest times often lead
to the greatest moments of your
life. Keep going. Tough situations
build strong people in the end.

⊙ *POETS CAFE*

June 13, 2023

You are a fighter. Look at
everything that you have
overcome. Don't give up.

⊙ *POETS CAFE*

June 14, 2023

In the depths of darkness, remember
this: the night is a canvas where stars
are born. Your struggles and pain may
seem overwhelming now, but within you
lies an unwavering resilience waiting to
be unleashed.
Embrace your journey, for it is through
adversity that we find our true strength.
Just as the dawn breaks and banishes
the shadows, so too shall you rise from
the depths and shine brighter than ever
before. POETS CAFE

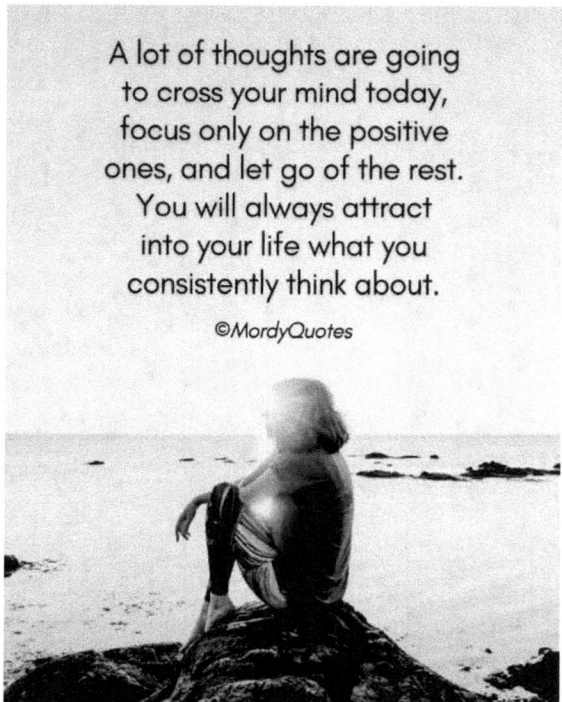

A lot of thoughts are going
to cross your mind today,
focus only on the positive
ones, and let go of the rest.
You will always attract
into your life what you
consistently think about.

©MordyQuotes

Learning how to believe in yourself will open up new endless possibilities in your life.

~ Unknown

Positive Inspirations With Dee Waldeck

Live Your Life on Purpose. Seize every opportunity to touch someone with Kindness.

The Kindness Cloud
KindnessCloud.org

What you go through
Each day doesn't
Define your worth.
Never let a bad day be the
Excuse to
Stop trying. Better
Days are coming and
Always remember that
You are worthy and enough

EXERCISE NOT ONLY
CHANGES YOUR BODY.
IT CHANGES YOUR
MIND, ATTITUDE,
AND MOOD.

they told me I couldn't,

that's why I did.

There is only one way
to guarantee things get better
in your life:

It is NOT by controlling
what happens OUTSIDE of you,

It is by mastering
what happens **WITHIN YOU.**

@IAMFEARLESSSOUL

The Kindness Cloud
KindnessCloud.org

NEVER LOOK DOWN ON ANYBODY UNLESS YOU'RE HELPING THEM UP.

September 30th, 2023

Today marked my initial read-through of the complete manuscript of this book. In anticipation of giving the green light for the release, the impact was unexpectedly powerful, compelling me to integrate this particular page, despite being only 10 days away from the official release. I wanted to share with you my immense sense of pride for Kimberley and Kaitlyn, not only for embarking on the journey of becoming authors and co-writing this book with me but also for their bravery and strength in sharing profoundly personal stories with all of you. Drawing from my own experiences of poverty, domestic abuse, and single parenthood, which I have shared in previous books and speaking engagements, it took me years to summon the courage to reveal my struggles. These young women bravely set aside their own pain to add details about their lives to this book that were traumatic and challenging to navigate. However, they stand strong, having conquered much adversity in their youth and shared their experiences in the hope of inspiring others to realize they too can overcome difficult circumstances and emerge as truly unstoppable individuals. I have unwavering confidence that Kimberley and Kaitlyn will continue to empower others to recognize the power within themselves. I consider myself incredibly blessed to call these two remarkable young women my daughters. Together, we proudly stand as survivors, committed to lifting others up as we strive towards reaching our own potential.

With much love and pride,
Cindy Witteman

Kimberley Witteman

Mother of two

https://www.facebook.com/profile.php?id=100093090483022
https://cfviews.com/kimberley-witteman

My name is Kimberley Witteman and I am 24 years old. I am a mom of two beautiful kids and a wife to an amazing husband. I currently work from home as a customer service representative. I've been in this line of work for almost a year. Before being a customer service representative I worked with my mother-in-law who owns her own business working on houses and I absolutely loved working with her; working with her was the best job I've ever had. I really hope that reading this book helps you understand you have every tool you need to have all the things you dream about.

CHAPTER 1
MIND OVER MATTER

My Story

If you have found your way to this book, you are meant to be here. You probably know or want to know about manifesting and how positive thinking can bring you what you desire... I mean, you're here reading this now, and I manifested you.

Content advisory: The chapters that follow include narratives that address sensitive subjects related to sexual assault.

To give you more of an understanding of me and my story, I am a mom to two beautiful kids: Dustin (4 years old) and Paisley (9 months old). I am also a wife to an amazing husband named Jacob. We have been together, on and off, for eight years. My life has never been easy and I am completely okay with it—I am proud of my life and where it has brought me. So with that being said, my story starts off at 14 years old. I have an amazing friend that I've had for years; we will call her Laura for the purpose of this story. Laura was everything I looked up to: She was beautiful, confident, courageous, and truly the best friend anybody could ask for (and she still is). Laura had a mom who pushed her to do and be her best; she was truly a great mom, just like my own. Laura also has a dad and two brothers, which I've never had. It was truly great that I had two families. I spent so much time with Laura and her family. We went to volleyball tournaments all the time; Laura's mom would fix her hair in braids, and her braids always came out so nice and beautiful! However, the happiness and joy was very short lived. Being a young, naïve little girl and not having a father, I didn't know how fathers were supposed to act or how they were supposed to take care of you. Laura's father took advantage of her; he would often come into her room after she was asleep and cuddle her inappropriately. I have never slept well at anybody's house but my own, so when I would spend the night Laura's dad would come and lay in between us and touch both of us inappropriately. I didn't know it was wrong—I thought dads were supposed to check to make sure everything was okay, and since he knew I didn't have a dad I assumed he was being kind enough to take care of me as well.

"THERE IS NOTHING IMPOSSIBLE TO THEY WHO WILL TRY." —ALEXANDER THE GREAT

Finally one morning I asked Laura why he did that every night. She informed me that it was something he has done since she was a little girl. I didn't think much of it after that, until one day I came over to get house to hangout with her and the doors to her closet and her bedroom were missing. Of course I asked what happened, and all she told me was she had locked her door to get dressed and her father got upset and took her doors off because he tried to come in and the door was locked. I told her my mom always knocks before trying to come in my room and always waited for a response before coming in. This is when I started to realize something wasn't right.

A couple years go by and I am now 16 years old. Things progressively got worse with Laura's father. I was so lost in myself and Laura's father threatened that if I were to say anything he would hurt my family. Despite everything going on in my life I still went to school; I started hanging out with Laura's youngest brother (we will call him Thomas). Thomas and I became close friends, and as my youngest sister had a crush on him, I tried my hardest to get them to date. Suddenly, I found myself falsely accused of having feelings for him, despite the fact that I didn't. I simply didn't want anyone to discover what was going on with Laura's father. Shortly after that I met my soon-to-be husband, Jacob, and we started to hang out all the time. Laura was pulled from our high school and moved to another school, so I was truly stuck by myself with nobody who understood me or what we were going through.

Things began to pick up with Jacob and I started telling him what was going on with Laura's father. He was very concerned and told me it wasn't right. I begged him not to say anything—I didn't want the backlash of people telling me "You asked for it," even though I didn't, or asking "What were you wearing?" when all I owned were jeans and t-shirts. Jacob never looked at me differently or asked me any questions like that. Since 14 years old I unknowingly had started manifesting Jacob into my life.

Jacob is a strong man and loves with his whole body. I stopped hanging out with Laura and hung out more with Jacob and his family. For a while I tried my best to forget everything that had happened to me.

I would cry just at the thought of it; he understood and never pushed me into anything. He was truly the man I always wanted.

My next manifestations were to build my family. I wanted a boy first, then a girl, and I always wanted justice for what happened to Laura and me. The years unfolded, and at 19 years old I gave birth to my handsome son Dustin. We were living with my husband's amazing family. Jacob's mom, Sunny, was super supportive and always there for me when I needed help. Sunny really opened my eyes to everything my mom had been telling me for years—your thoughts become your reality. Sunny taught me about all kinds of things I didn't even know existed. She also let me work for her; she owed a handy woman business. Honestly, it is still the best job I have ever had. While we worked together we got super close and we talked about things we've never told anybody else. Jacob and I broke up quite a few times during our eight years together, and every time something happened I always had Sunny. She always told me she knew we were meant to be together and one day we would get married. She was definitely right.

Fast forward six months—I was contacted by the police department at which I had made a report two years prior. They had called me to see when I was available to speak about what had happened to me. I informed the detective I didn't have a working vehicle but she could come to me. She showed up that same day at my job with no discretion; she came in full uniform and asked for me by name. The detective took me to the police station and recorded my statement. Afterward she took me home, where my husband met me with a bunch of questions oaboutn why I was dropped off in a police car, and I finally told him the whole situation. The next day Laura's father was taken to jail. They had enough evidence to charge him, and that was so scary to me because I had a family now—I didn't want him to find me and hurt them.

At 23 years old, having just given birth to my daughter, I was notified that he had plead guilty to all charges. My manifestation had been completed and I felt that my kids and I were safe. My next manifestation was that Jacob and I would get married. This manifestation that I have waited a long time for recently came true when Jacob asked me to marry him. I was so pleased and super grateful. It's so crazy and bizarre that the things you think about can come true like this. But I am really proud of myself and all the challenges I have overcome to get here.

Today on my manifestation list I have: buying my first home, owning a 2024 Dodge 2500, and going on a vacation to Oklahoma. I can't wait to see where your manifestations take you!

GETTING STARTED

A positive mindset doesn't happen overnight. It takes time; studies show it takes 30 days to break a bad habit. So be patient with yourself; it's time we replace the negative with the positive, and know you're not alone. Make sure you continue to read with an open mind; everything you hear today will sound like complete bullshit but it is 100% the truth. I've personally done everything in this article. If it can work for me, it can work for you!

Manifesting is a way of thinking, just like positive thinking. When manifesting, you need to remember: "I think," "I feel," " I have," " I am." This takes hard work and patience with yourself and with others. There is no right or wrong way to manifest the things you "already" have in your life, which means you get the leeway to use any way that feels right to you.

To start, let's look more closely at positive thoughts.

Positivity is a work in progress, but we must be positive to manifest what we "have." You can always start your day off with great thoughts before you even get out of bed. For example, simply thinking "Today is going to be a great day." Or when you go to brush your teeth, "I am strong. I am kind. I am beautiful. I am enough. I am loved." You will notice a huge change in the way you feel just by starting your day off with self-positivity. You can also end your day with positivity: "Today was great but tomorrow will be better!" Or, "I am so grateful for everything I have and much more." If you're going through a rough patch in your day, it's ok to take a mental break and recenter yourself in your mind. It's ok to feel—we are all human. I have rough days too; don't let anybody try to fool you! Being positive is hard and it's a lot of work especially when you're first starting out. Just remember that the more you feel positive the more you will be positive. I know because it works for me!

At first you will feel like you're fighting your mind. If you stay diligent throughout this process, you will overcome those negative thoughts. Remember this takes time—just remember "I think. I feel. I have. I am." When manifesting, this will help you focus on the current dream. You will eventually be able to recognize a negative thought and correct it with something positive, without even thinking. For example, your brain will automatically change "My tire blew while going to work and I was 5 minutes late!" to "My tire blew, but I made it to work safe." Just by making little changes in your thinking you will notice a huge difference in how the days to come will unfold and change your everyday life. Being aware of your subconscious thoughts will come over time, but if you are already aware then you're ahead of the game! A subconscious thought can come at anytime and in any situation. Correcting them is where it feels like you are fighting with your mind. I know, I hear you loud and clear—asking how one thought can change your whole day. Think about it for a minute. I bet we've all been in a hard time where we really needed or wanted something. We will focus on that need or want with all of our might, then all of a sudden things work out and we receive what we've been needing or wanting. This is what I like to call the laws of attraction.

The laws of attraction is a philosophy claiming that one's thoughts determine their reality. So, the more you think about the things you "have," the quicker they come to you. Remember that the dreams you are thinking about you have already received. You're not waiting to get this dream, but grateful you have already received it. Being grateful is the biggest thing you can do for the universe—most times people just expect. I am sure we have all met somebody like that and we do not appreciate it. It's always good to thank the universe for giving us our true desires, just like we thank a person for giving us a gift. When showing appreciation the person on the receiving end feels happy and positive. Show your positivity and share it with others.

One day in the near future you will become aware of your thoughts, which will make correcting them a lot easier. A good way to offset negative feelings is by playing some music that makes you feel good; my go to is upbeat music that makes me happy. Your mind and thoughts control everything in your life, so let go of the bad and turn it into a lesson for the future. Always make sure you acknowledge how your mindset is already changing and give yourself credit where it's due because you deserve it. You've got this! You are strong. You are kind. You are beautiful. You are enough. You are loved. Feeling and being positive makes you stand out in a crowd. Your positive light will shine so bright, you might just blind the person next to you! Not literally but you know what I mean. Don't be afraid to share that positivity and confidence, more people than you think could really use that!

Now that we are thinking more positive, we can talk about manifesting.

Manifesting is a way of thinking, being, becoming, and having. My mom has been my biggest rock when it comes to manifesting and positive thinking; she once told me that wanting something isn't enough—you need to imagine, believe, and feel in order to receive. Oh man was she right! Just stick to it, it may not happen overnight but it is worth it in the end. For instance, I've been manifesting a raise at work to $24/hour for over a year. Just over two weeks ago, I received a call that my campaign was ending. I was so sad and so upset but my sister was there to help me stay positive and motivated for things to come. A couple days after, I received another call—I was getting promoted, which would come with an eight dollar increase hourly. At the time I didn't think about it—I was still upset about the campaign ending—but once I took the time to step back and calculate how much I was going to make an hour, I realized I'd made it to my $24/hour manifestation. So be persistent and your life will change; it'll come in the most unexpected ways, but will come when you need it the most.

Manifesting might not be an overnight thing, but make sure you imagine it, feel it, and believe you already have it while remaining positive. I myself struggle a lot with self-doubt and it's hard for me to believe I deserve anything that I currently have, which makes it really hard for me to manifest my true desires. It was hard to overcome this obstacle. Honestly, I let the self-doubt control a lot of my life. One day, I said, *this cannot be my life*. I knew I was meant to do something bigger than myself, so I picked myself up and never let the little voice in the back of my head tell me I cannot do it, I cannot have it, because I can have anything I want and I can have anything I manifest. So if you have the little voice like I do, prove it wrong. I know you can! We are a lot alike, feeling scared and a bit out of place. Just know you are always welcome here!

Personally, I have manifested a lot of things in my life and some still haven't come true yet; you need to be very specific about what you desire. If not, the universe has a funny way of giving you what you want and what you're asking for in just a different way. For instance, I manifested winning the lottery. I wasn't specific about an amount or anything, but I did win the lottery... $4 for matching a couple numbers. Even though that's not exactly what I wanted, that's exactly what I asked for! You might think your desire is too crazy to receive or maybe you don't feel worthy enough. Just remember, I believe in you, and I believe you are worth more than anything in this world. You have the power to manifest anything you want (within reason, people probably won't turn into squirrels or minions). I also don't want you to think we can only manifest items—we can also manifest confidence, ideas, etc. Don't confine your manifestations to just objects—manifest your mind.

I want to tell you a little secret about myself… I struggle a lot with severe anxiety and self-doubt. This has held me back so much in my life. When I first learned about being positive and manifesting, I could not do it because of all the anxiety and self-doubt I had about what people would think, what people might say or even what I might say to myself. Because of my anxiety and self-doubt, I have this little voice in the back of my head telling me, "You'll never get that!" or, "Yeah right, like that's even possible!" or maybe even, "You don't deserve that!" That is the reason why I believe positivity always comes before manifesting, because with confidence you can turn your dreams into reality, just like I have! I myself can vouch for manifesting because it has changed my life and it can change yours.

If it weren't for my mom, I would not be here today telling you how manifesting has changed my life. She has been there for me throughout all of the rough patches in my life. When I was younger, I would complain about everything. Trust me, if there was something to complain about, I would, instead of taking responsibility and fixing it. My mom would always remind me that the more negatively I spoke, the more negative things would come to me. Honestly I thought *yeah right, my life is just this way because it's meant to be this way.* I would think that if I took five minutes out of my week to beg for my life to change it would happen overnight. That was not the case, and I would get so discouraged and tell her it wasn't real. So I finally took the time to listen to what she had said and took a couple months to get my head straight and give manifesting a fair chance and I am so glad I did. I definitely needed those months to learn to be grateful for my life and everything I had in it. I also evaluated my life and everything that I have brought to myself, and I realized she was so right. The more I spoke about the negative things in my life the more negative things came. So I started taking her advice. I watched the show that she recommended and from then on, I decided I have control of my own life. I have control over what happens in my life.

But in my young mind, it was very hard to understand that thoughts, words, and feelings could bring things into reality. I also deflected a lot of my problems onto other people instead of taking responsibility for what I had brought on myself. I learned to take responsibility because in all reality, I did bring this on myself. Let me tell you this doesn't make the journey easy; still to this day I have to correct those bad thoughts. I will say that the more you do it, the more it becomes second nature.

It took a lot of self-awareness to take that knowledge and grow from it. Isn't that what life is all about, learning things for yourself, growing and becoming the person you are truly meant to be? Well, at least that is what life means to me. I would love to say that once I learned to take responsibility for my actions my life changed easily, but that's not the case… I had to work hard to get through all the negative thoughts I had already put into action and at the same time put positive thoughts into place for the future. "I am strong. I am kind. I am beautiful. I am enough. I am loved." The road ahead might be tough but I know if anybody can do this it's YOU! I can't wait to see the all the things you accomplish in this lifetime.

You are kind. You are strong. You are beautiful. You are loved. You are enough!

Let those words ring in your head. I am right here with you and you deserve more than you are giving yourself. Remember, you can and will make all of your dreams reality, just like I did!

I want to explain a little bit about the things that helped me achieve my overall positivemindset. My mother-in-law helped me so much, and you wouldn't believe what an amazingly bright, kind, caring, brave, courageous, and take-no-shit kind of person she is. I mean, it's only fitting that her name is Sunny.

Sunny taught me that I can clean my energy and space of unwanted and unkind energy. Sunny didn't only tell me this—she showed me in her home. Let me tell you, when she pulled out this bundle of what looked to be some kind of small, dried-up plant I thought, "Umm what are we going to do with that?" But I didn't even speak; I had to remind myself to have an open mind and know she wouldn't show me something that she didn't try herself. She took me to the living room and told me to open the window. Then she explained that we can sage all day but the bad energy wouldn't be able to leave if it had no way out. Then I asked, "Is that sage?" She laughed and said "Yes hunny, it is." She then continued to explain that there are multiple different kinds of "smudge sticks or herb bundles." Once again I was lost but continued to listen attentively; I needed a change and I was willing to try anything that might help. Then we walked to the furthest room from the window and lit the sage. She began to say, "Any negative energy or evil spirits in my home, you are not welcome here. You need to leave out the window. Now." As she said this over and over I started to say it with her. As soon as I got the hang of it she handed me the sage and I finished throughout all the rooms and closets. It's important to get every area so that everything is clean. She took me by the window and I handed her the sage, assuming we were done. She informed me we were not done, we had to seal all doors and windows. "We don't want the negative to be able to come back in!" This created protection so the negative couldn't enter unless with another person. She said, "It doesn't work on men, I already tried it with Curtis." Let me tell you, she loves to give her husband a hard time. We laughed and so did he.

"Babe, you can't get rid of me that easy," he said, and gave her a kiss. I could definitely notice a change in the feeling in the house. It all just felt light and airy. Kind of like when you're at peace at home snuggled up in your bed reading a book. After she finished she had me go outside with her and then she started to sage me, saying, "Any negative energy please leave her alone. She deserves the utmost positivity and clarity." It was probably the most awkward experience I've ever had. But I still felt so much better and more positive. She also gave me her last stick of Palo Santo, which helps bring in positivity, and a bundle of my own sage.

The next time I saw her she started telling me about different types of crystals and what they help with. I came to find out they can help with manifesting! Different crystals can help you manifest money, love, prosperity, confidence, and much more. So we went crystal hunting at different stores, which is definitely not a cheap thing to do. But we got one of each crystal with the cards that go with them so I could learn which one was the correct one to use at each time. She also bought me a bracelet with all the chakras. Don't be like me and get lost during this process. Everybody has chakras; there is a crown, third eye, throat, heart, solar, sacral, and root chakra. Working with your chakras brings all of your energy together to help you work at your best level. This is something that Sunny's mother-in-law taught her. She has used this for years and it has helped her to become her highest self. I haven't reached that yet, but I am working toward it.

Sunny also taught me about candles and how they can help me manifest. A white candle can be used in place of any color if that particular candle isn't available. A blue candle can be used for meditation, loyalty, spiritual protection, overcoming addiction, inner peace, and trauma. A red candle can be used for energy, courage, fertility, passion and lust, negativity and pessimism, and strength. A purple candle can be used to enhance psychic ability, astral travel, wisdom, ambition, insomnia, and bad karma. A yellow candle can be used for confidence, optimism, charm, communication, good luck, and concentration. A green candle is used to help manifest wealth and prosperity. A pink candle is used for romance, friendship, spiritual healing, self-love, faith, and forgiveness. An orange candle can be used for stamina, success, prosperity, youthfulness, sudden changes, and independence. A black candle is used for protection, reverse hexes/curses, absorbing negative energy, revealing secrets, loss and grief support, and illness. A gold candle can be used for abundance, happiness, awareness and knowledge, influence, divination, and power. A silver candle can be used for astral realm, ambition, fame, purity, communication with ancestors, and creativity. A grey candle can be used for imagination, visions, wisdom, psychic protection, patience, and obstacles. This helped me so much and also helped me focus on one type of manifestation rather than trying to overwhelm myself with everything at one time. There are also things like protection jars to help protect against negativity, but protection jars can be used for all different kinds of protection or to bring things to you. This honestly opened up a whole new world me. Tarot cards, pendulums, spirit guides, and even green witch spells. With an open mind, I started researching and learned about so many amazing things that have always been right here at my fingertips and I just didn't know it. These things are so interesting to me; why is it that nobody really talks about how many things we can do to benefit our current situations? For instance, you can blow cinnamon in your front door to help bring wealth and prosperity into your home. Or you can cleanse your home and space with sage (white, red, black, blue), cedar, lavender, desert, Yerba Santa, rosemary, juniper and Palo Santo. Well, you will find it here because I believe everybody should have the knowledge to help them on their journey. It might not be the same as mine so you don't need to feel pressured to take everything; feel free to take some and leave some. Do your own research and decide what fits into your life. Just take some advice from me; a lot of people have closed minds and will treat you differently just for talking about the things you've found to work. Just remember, "You are kind. You are smart. You are beautiful. You are strong. You are enough." You will always be all of those things no matter what other people think. Misery loves company and you will not be that company because you are worth more and you deserve better. I am here to show you that like any other path that has the potential to change your life, it takes a lot of hard work and patience.

Now let's talk a little bit about meditation. I believe calming and centering yourself helps with manifesting. With that being said, you need to be completely focused on what you have and how you feel. Don't you get worried now—you don't have to meditate by sitting crisscross on the floor in complete silence, humming and doing hand movements. Meditation can be sitting quietly in your room or listening to your favorite music. Whatever makes you feel the most focused, calm, and ready for change, putting yourself in the mindset that you can have everything you can think of.

AFFIRMATIONS

I also want to share with you some different affirmations that help manifestation and should be said several times a day.

This affirmation is for money and has to be said three times a day for seven days for you to notice a change. "I always have more money than I need. I cannot help but attract money into my life."

This is an affirmation for self confidence which and has to be said several times a day: "I am confident, I am perfect, I trust myself, I love myself for everything I am and I let go of perfection—good enough is ok."

In terms of affirmations for positivity, this is a great one to start off with: "I choose to be happy, I have everything I need to succeed, my dreams are coming true, I can get through everything and I am grateful for all that I have."

Affirmations for love: "I am letting love into my life, I deserve fulfilling relationships, I attract trustworthy and loving relationships and I deserve love as I am."

"I am powerful and control my own reality, I attract all that is good in the universe, I find myself in a state of perpetual happiness."

"Today I am the best version of myself. I am ready to achieve my goals. I am thankful for this day and grateful for new opportunities. I love and accept this mind and this body. I will nourish and cherish them through loving thoughts, today and always."

"Regardless of my past I am worthy of loving myself. Regardless of how others view me I view myself as worthy of change and forgiveness, I stand firm in valuing myself."

"I prove to myself everyday that I can become the person of my dreams, my true self for everyone to see."

Affirmations can help manifest anything and you can always turn them into something of your own. I have chills because I am so excited to see where you take all this information I've given. Again, there is no right or wrong way to use affirmations in a positive way, so mix them up, use them together, and get your dreams out there. I believe in you so much and I know you're going to do great things after you read this book. Take your time, vibe out, listen to music, and never let anybody touch your positive progress. I am manifesting great things for you because you deserve a change. Work hard and get your mind ready to receive the things you already have. I am proud of you. I love you. I know you are strong, kind, beautiful, enough, deserving, and I know you are trying! Be the kind and courageous person I know you are and go conquer your dreams and be proud of the person you're becoming!

If you would like to start your own manifesting journal, here is a guide to help you with that process.

What you have already:

_____

_____

_____

_____

_____

How does having this make you feel?

_____

_____

_____

_____

_____

How has this changed your life?

_____

_____

_____

_____

_____

Express how grateful and thankful you are for this:

_____

_____

_____

_____

_____

List everything you are grateful for in your life:

1. _____

2. _____

3. _____

4. _____

5. _____

And so on, even list simple things like your pen and paper. You need to be truly grateful and thankful for the things you have. The extra things will come.

Inspirational quotes chosen by Kimberley Witteman

You don't tell a story only to yourself.
There's always someone else.
Even when there is no one.

—Margaret Atwood, The Handmaid's Tale

But right now, I'm content to bask in the sun and glory of the world that is my own.

—Seeker

There is music that's free, that will surely
beguile "Tis the song of the bird as he sings,
And the sun-kissed breeze makes us linger
awhile
Just to look for the beautiful things.
Let us close our eyes to the faults of a friend
Drop them deep in oblivion's springs,
As we travel along to life's golden end
We can always find beautiful things.

—Lucile B. Ballard

The past is what you were not what you are

—K. Tolnoe

Perhaps the light that made her beautiful was not from her eyes, nor from her smile, but from the way that no matter the darkness that swirled around her, within her,
she still found the courage to shine.

—Mandy Antoniacci

Once you replace negative thoughts with positive ones, you'll start having positive results.

—Willie Nelson

You cannot have a positive life
and a negative mind.

—Joyce Meyer

MAGIC IS
BELIEVING IN
YOURSELF
If you can make that happen, you can make
anything happen.

—Johann Wolfgang Von Goethe

Don't let the expectations and opinions of other people affect your decisions. It's your life, not theirs. Do what matters most to you; do what makes you feel alive and happy.

Don't let the expectations and ideas of others limit who you are. If you let others tell you who you are, you are living their reality—not yours. There is more to life than pleasing people.

There is much more to life than following others' prescribed path. There is so much more to life than what you experience right now. You need to decide who you are for yourself. Become a whole being. Adventure.

—Roy T. Bennett

Sometimes the bad things that happen in our lives put us directly on the path to the best things that will ever happen to
US.

—Nicole Reed

"Our greatest weakness lies in giving up. The most certain way to succeed is always to try just one more time."

—Thomas Edison

Kaitlyn Chavez

Mom

https://www.facebook.com/kaitlyn.myshell
https://cfviews.com/kaitlyn-chavez

My name is Kaitlyn Chavez. I'm 25 years old and very family-oriented. I have been married since 2020 and have a beautiful baby girl. I was in the Texas Army National Guard as a Financial Management Technician for six years from the age of 17-23. During my career, I was deployed once and volunteered to go on COVID-19 orders. During my time in the military, I did everything I could to go above and beyond to help people. I was coined several times for figuring out the solution to problems that were being overlooked. My goal was never to get glory. I simply just wanted to help. That's what I am here to do today. I want to help you overcome negativity and start manifesting your life.

CHAPTER 1
HOW MANIFESTING CHANGED MY LIFE

Introduction

In the chapters that lie ahead, I am not only going to address the question of "Is Manifesting Bullshit?" which is on many minds, but also invite you to join me in a detailed account of my personal experiences. This journey weaves through the challenges, the moments of pain, and the burdens of stress that I dealt with. These very experiences became the gateway to my ability to understand how manifestation truly works. What's even more exciting is that, together, we will uncover the essential steps required to effectively harness the power of manifestation in your life, regardless of where you have been or where you currently stand in your journey.

Content advisory: The chapters that follow include narratives that address sensitive subjects related to sexual assault.

Initially, when I was introduced to the concept of manifesting, I dismissed it as a waste of time and thought it was completely bogus. How could just thinking positively and believing in what I am saying change my life? I believed it all to be bullshit. Little did I know just how much negative thinking was hurting my life. This chapter goes into detail about how manifesting and positive thinking showed themselves and transformed my life.

From the time I was a young kid all the way through middle school, I had self-doubts about who I was and why I wasn't good enough. My father wasn't in my life from a very young age, and that contributed to my feelings of worthlessness. How could I expect to find love and happiness when my own father did not want me? This only got worse as I progressed further in my education and experienced bullying. My thoughts were drowning in negativity and all the hurtful words spoken by people in my high school dragged me down. I heard the ringing of what was spoken in my head constantly, persistent and loud: "You are not good enough, you are not strong enough, you are not skinny enough, you are not beautiful enough, you are not smart enough."

It got to the point where I believed their words so strongly that I started to tear myself down, looking at pictures of myself and saying every hurtful thing imaginable. Things like, "I'm five foot five and one hundred and twenty pounds, my tummy is too big. I need to lose ten pounds," and "Oh no, they are taking a photo of me, I need to suck it in and take my glasses off," or "I'm such a four-eyed nerd but I'm so stupid, why can't I just be like the popular girls?" This eventually became, "I'm so ugly, the only time anybody is ever going to notice me is when they are laughing at me," and even, "I am not worthy of love."

During this time, I had a job working as a Host at Chili's. I was only 17 so I was too young to be a server. I had a boyfriend who we will call Steve for the purpose of this story. Steve and I started dating freshman year, and I was so in love with him. I thought we would be together forever, get married, and even have kids. We both made mistakes, and one day we got into a fight and broke up. I was devastated. I had so many sleepless nights just crying and tearing myself apart. Then, finally, I decided that it was time to get up and deal with my sadness. Looking back on it now, I will admit that I definitely did not go about it the right way. If I had known about and believed in manifesting at the time, maybe I would not have allowed myself to be so overtaken by negativity.

One day I went to Texas Roadhouse to have dinner with my mom and my jaw dropped when I saw our server. He was tall with a deep, booming voice, and I thought he was so handsome. I didn't say anything to him but told my mom I thought he was hot when he walked away. I thought nothing of it, because why would a handsome man want anything to do with me? After we left, though, he managed to get my number, and sometime later, I received an unexpected text message. He told me how beautiful he thought I was and how he would like to take me on a date.

I immediately jumped into a relationship with him after just meeting. On our first couple of dates, he was the perfect gentleman—I had fallen into his trap. It didn't take long for him to start trying to control me. It started as, "Please don't wear that," then, "You aren't allowed to talk to anyone except me." One time I did not answer the phone because I was in the shower, and he screamed at me when I called him back.

Shortly after, we went to Six Flags for a date. During a safety check, the attendant unintentionally brushed my thigh with the back of his hand. It was just a routine task, yet I found myself in trouble for not pulling away. This left me baffled; I was securely strapped in, and the attendant was merely performing his duties. There was no inappropriate intent or flirtation involved. He had simply adjusted the belt and moved on with his tasks. I attempted to explain this to him, but he remained indifferent. His only desire seemed to be for me to react with disgust, despite the employee's innocence.

Deep inside, I began to realize that I deserved better. I had assumed that such incidents were somehow a normal part of a relationship, whatever "normal" meant. However, my mother opened my eyes to the fact that this behavior wasn't healthy. With newfound clarity, I made the difficult decision to end the relationship. Strangely enough, even though our time together had only lasted two weeks, things had escalated rapidly. While I hadn't reached the stage of being in love, the breakup was still painful.

This was a reminder that the duration of a relationship doesn't always correlate with the depth of emotions felt. Sometimes, even in a short span, we encounter situations that lead us to make important realizations and difficult choices.

As I entered a new phase of life, I found myself drawn to a different crowd, one that didn't necessarily have the best reputation. Believing that they could relate to my experiences and that we shared a similar outlook, I began spending more time with them. Little did I know that this decision would set off a chain of events that would deeply impact my wellbeing.

This shift in friendship had broader implications than I initially realized. Over time, I started making choices that weren't in my best interest, both for my physical health and for my mental state. What's more, I began to adopt some of the attitudes and behaviors of these newfound acquaintances, which marked a significant departure from the person I had always been.

Before this phase, my life had been characterized by responsibility and adherence to rules. I was known as someone who made sound choices and followed a straight path. However, everything seemed to change once I crossed paths with this new circle.

Almost everyone in this group was considerably older than I was, and this included the person I began dating, who was a 23-year-old. Unfortunately, his influence began to steer me toward activities that I had never previously engaged in. He consistently encouraged me to indulge in activities like smoking marijuana and drinking excessively, activities that seemed to come with a sense of excitement and rebellion. I found myself giving in, which ultimately resulted in me neglecting my responsibilities at home and even skipping school.

Strangely enough, even though the actions were spurred by his influence, I felt a deep sense of guilt and blamed myself for the consequences that followed. It's only now, in retrospect, that I recognize the complexity of the situation. At 17, I was still in the midst of navigating the challenges of adolescence, while he was a full-fledged adult. Clearly, the power dynamics were skewed in his favor, and he took advantage of my vulnerability.

Despite the red flags that might have been apparent to others, I was blinded by a perception of newfound excitement and thrill. The notion of "fun" clouded my judgment, causing me to overlook the potential risks and consequences that came with the choices I was making. In the midst of all this, I failed to recognize the importance of safeguarding my own wellbeing and making choices that truly aligned with my values and long-term goals.

I was completely unaware that my low self-image was ruining my life. It's astonishing to think about how my thoughts slowly but surely began to destroy me. The consequences of this mindset manifested in multiple areas: my inability to pass drug tests, my declining grades as I failed classes, and perhaps most alarming of all, my entanglement in a relationship that was predatory and harmful.

Luckily, my mom intervened, despite my resistance. She was determined to ensure that the 23-year-old responsible for exploiting me faced legal consequences for his actions. My perspective was entirely different at the time—I was practically begging her not to take action against this person. Even though I wasn't entirely forthcoming with her, I tried to convey that I had made a conscious decision to be part of that situation, in an attempt to convince her there was no coercion or manipulation involved.

In the aftermath, it became painfully evident that the person in question was a serial exploiter. I was completely shocked to find out that, within a mere week of our breaking up, this individual had already targeted a new victim, another 17-year-old. Hindsight has provided me with a clearer view: This individual was undoubtedly a predator who understood exactly what he was doing. He intentionally leveraged the age difference to manipulate and take advantage of vulnerable individuals like us. Looking back, it became apparent that my mom was right in wanting to take legal measures to prevent such actions from continuing.

My mom forced me to quit my job. Seeing the disappointment on her face made me decide to start making the right decisions for myself. She started speaking to me about manifesting and how it could change my life.

"Ok, Mom," I said, while simultaneously thinking, "What a load of bullshit. I'll show her that all you have to do is work hard, not manifest, to make what you want a reality." I just needed to find something to teach me stability and discipline.

I started going back to school and had to work hard to bring my GPA back up so that I could graduate on time. I stayed after hours and went to a study group. I even went as far as asking for extra credit and makeup work. Slowly my grades started rising and I was so proud of the positive progress I was making.

In the middle of all of my hard work a Staff Sergeant recruiter came in to talk to us about careers in the Texas Army National Guard. I knew I needed a reality check and saw joining as my opportunity. This was it. This was what I needed to get myself on the right track and become a better person. I decided that this was what I wanted to do to change for the better. Because I was only 17 years old and didn't have a diploma, I needed way better grades, a good ASVAB score, and my mom's permission to join.

Step one was to get my grades up. I turned in all of my makeup hours, makeup work, and extra credit. After all of that, I turned my failing GPA into a passing one through all of my hard work and determination. I felt incredibly proud and excited to be back on track, knowing that I would graduate with my class.

Step two was to take the ASVAB and score higher than 31. I studied for hours, took practice tests, and asked for all the help I could get. Once I was scoring high enough on my practice tests it was time to take the real deal. With sweaty palms and a hopeful mind, I walked into the testing room. I finished the test, breathed a sigh of relief, and went to get my score. I did it! I got twice the score needed to join. Excited, I told my mom and saw how proud she was of my positive transformation.

Then came the toughest step: convincing my mom. She wanted to be sure that joining the Texas Army National Guard was the right choice; she needed all the facts before saying yes. After doing research and demonstrating to her that it was the best option, she remained uncertain. I arranged a meeting with the recruiter to address her questions. With persistence, I convinced her to sign the documents with me.

Things progressed quickly, and after getting approval, I needed to undergo a physical by an army physician before my swearing-in. Once that was done, I was able to consider my career choices. I had two options: parachute packer or Financial Management Technician. I decided to opt for the latter, focusing on the potential of the finance field. Then came the swearing-in ceremony. Taking the oath with my hand raised, I became a fresh recruit; I had successfully completed this step. I was finally prepared to fulfill my six-year contract of service.

I started the Recruit Sustainment Program (RSP), joining others who had also enlisted, and we attended training one weekend per month. RSP is training prior to boot camp only available for those of us who joined the National Guard or the reserves. I started learning the commands, getting in shape, and taking mock Physical Training (PT) tests. I kept a positive outlook, believing this was the most beneficial path for me. I became more willing to cooperate within reason, and my sense of gratitude expanded. It was as if my mind had opened up to a whole new world of understanding. I was changing and growing with every second that passed. I liked my job and volunteered often to learn more and become better prepared. I found myself featured in a magazine as the representative of my National Guard unit, with an article written by my leadership about me. I also received a promotion for all of my hard work before boot camp even started. I noticed my body was changing and I was in the best shape of my life. My confidence was slowly increasing and so was my happiness.

Here is where Steve came back into my life, and I hoped that this would make my dream of marrying my high school sweetheart come true. We started dating again and everything seemed to be going perfectly. I was happy again and thought that everything was falling into place. We sat and talked, I told him that I had joined the Texas Army National Guard and was going to boot camp in a couple of months. He was so confused that the girl he once knew had completely changed and was now so much more positive.

"You aren't the girl I used to know," he said. "You have changed and gotten stronger."

I shared the details of everything that had unfolded since our breakup, and he shouldered the blame for the challenges I had faced, saying, "If we hadn't broken up, maybe none of this would have happened." A few weeks later, we reunited for a memorable date and attended prom together. That night, we had an incredible time, and I experienced a rare sense of being free from worries. A couple of weeks after that, we graduated side by side.

Before we knew it, I was being shipped off. He came to my BMT graduation two months later and I was so excited to see him. But at the same time, I was so sad because I knew he would go back home while I had to stay another six weeks for my job training (AIT) as a Financial Management Technician. At least during AIT, I was allowed to have my phone so I could talk to him. One night while I was on the phone with him, I was scrolling through Instagram, and I saw a girl with a neck brace and mentioned it to him.

He remarked, "Oh, is that Susan?"

I answered, "Yeah, how do you know her? I have no idea who she is."

"Oh, she is no one, just someone I met while hanging out with the boys. It's crazy because she tripped over her own feet, falling and spraining her neck."

There was something odd about this. I thought, "If she's a nobody, why does he know the details, and why is she friends with me on Instagram?" Something felt fishy. So, I messaged her, and the awkward conversation ensued...

"Hi, my name is Kaitlyn, how do you know Steve?"

"Hi, nice to meet you. I know him because we met while I was serving him and his friends at Main Event. He asked me on a date, and I said yes. How do you know him?"

"He and I have been in a relationship for a few years. I want you to know that I'm not directing any anger toward you, I'm just trying to gather more information. I think he is cheating on me, so I just want the facts."

"Ok."

"When did y'all go on your date?"

Her dates matched a period when we were together. She apologized, claiming she didn't know he wasn't single, and said they had only kissed.

Of course, I confronted him, telling him, "I talked to Susan, and she told me everything."

He admitted, "It was only one night, it didn't mean anything," confirming my gut-wrenching suspicion of infidelity.

I asked, "Why?" His reply shattered my self-confidence and all the effort I had made to stay positive.

"You weren't good enough to wait for. I had urges, don't you understand?"

Despite this, I chose to work on the relationship, thinking, "Love conquers all, right?"

Once I graduated and was able to come back home, I saw my father for the first time. He held me and told me how much he loved me, and I broke down. I started spending more time with him and getting to know him. In reconnecting with him, I realized that I was never the problem. He did love me; he was just young and hadn't made the right decisions. So it truly was possible for me to be loved. I could have it all—I just had to believe that everything would work out in time.

Not long after reconnecting with my father, Steve and I ended our relationship. I discovered that he had continued to be unfaithful even after I gave him another chance. In an instant, it became clear that our relationship held no significance for him. Despite believing it was him and me against the world, I found out he was talking negatively about me to his friends, saying things like, "She's crazy and needs to lose weight." It turned out that all the time and effort I invested in our relationship meant nothing to him. I was essentially wasting my valuable time trying to salvage something that only I thought was worth fighting for.

I had many crying sessions, which allowed me to express my emotions. But was it really necessary for me to be that self-critical? Picking at every mistake I've made over the years like it was a scab, I was just opening the wound again. I spoke those words into existence and there was no taking them back. It made me realize that all of the harsh things I said to myself were coming true and that manifesting worked both ways. A negative mindset will be rewarded with a negative outcome and environment, and vice versa. Yes, you can apologize, but words are not so easily forgotten. Sometimes the worst cuts you can receive are not the ones that can be seen or healed leaving behind a scar; they are the ones that are trapped in your mind on repeat, cutting deeper and deeper with every thought. They are the ones spoken by yourself, a family member, a friend, or even a stranger. I wanted this negativity to disappear from my life. I had to change again.

It was time to make my dreams a reality. I was ready to try positive thinking. I woke up every morning and told myself out loud in the mirror, "I AM beautiful, I AM strong, I AM enough." I felt silly for the first couple of days, weeks even. Then I noticed it—the change was slow, gradual, and all at once. I started feeling strong, beautiful, and worthy. I am all of these things that I believe I am. I felt the growth boiling up inside so much that I felt like exploding.

Once I'd boosted my confidence, I was ready to start manifesting. I realized I had already been manifesting a major part of my life since I was a little girl: I would tell myself and anyone who would listen, "I want to be a mom when I grow up. I am going to meet someone in high school, we are going to fall in love, get married, and start a beautiful family. We will have a long and lasting marriage," and, "Love conquers all."

When I said this, I imagined that my husband and I would start to date in high school and the rest would follow from there. BOY, was I wrong! It turns out I wasn't specific enough with my manifestation. Looking back on it now, I got everything I asked for.

I met Russell my junior year of high school, and my best friend at the time had a crush on him. I already had a boyfriend, so I was more focused on trying to get him to date her. I admit that I had a crush on him, but to play it off I was mean to him. I graduated in 2016 and started my career in the Army. Three years later I ended up deploying to Qatar for ten months. When I came back home, I was on rest and relaxation orders. As the orders finished up, COVID started to devastate the world with shutdowns and deaths. I was activated and put with a team of amazingly positive people.

During the mission, I was tasked with supporting the medical team by giving COVID vaccinations to Texans. Even though this mission was not job-specific for me, I love to help. I started doing everything I could to make our task fast and efficient. I ended up getting "coined" (a military honor recognizing Army Excellence in Efficiency through Special Commemorative Coins) by a three-star general for all of the changes I made in order to help the team save resources and time.

We ended up having a lot of downtime between job sites. Luckily, I got to know every person on the team. I bonded with the group, and we became close friends. We all supported each other, shared our doubts, and found ways to uplift each other. When we would ask each other a question our answer was always "Send it," meaning if it will make you happy, then do it. The people I was now hanging out with were rubbing off on me and I was truly becoming a better version of myself.

One day I was bored and had expressed to them that I was ready to date again. They encouraged me to download a dating app. Even though I was skeptical at first—thinking that dating apps were only meant for hookups and not something real or long-lasting—I decided to download Tinder.

After a couple of days and lots of swiping, I saw his face.

"Russell??" I asked, excited.

"Kaitlyn??" he responded playfully.

We talked for a couple of weeks, and then he asked me on a date. At first I was still really iffy and didn't know what to expect. I did not want him to think I was an "easy girl," so I was debating saying no. He was stubborn and I kept using the excuse, "Finding a time isn't easy. I am being moved around from hotel to hotel in different cities to help with the vaccinations."

After a couple of weeks, I finally decided to go on a date with him. After all, someone with such persistence at least deserved a chance. We settled on Chester's, a burger joint in San Antonio, followed by a visit to the park.

While we were at the park, I turned to him and asked, "Why did you want to go on a date with me?"

His response was candid. "Well, when I see something I want, I go for it. When we first connected on Tinder, I just thought I was catching up with a familiar face from high school. Then I got to know you and realized you were really a great person, so I wanted to go on a date and see if we were actually a good match."

I revealed something unexpected, saying, "You know what's interesting? Back in high school, I actually had a crush on you. Unfortunately, I had a boyfriend and my best friend had already expressed interest in you, so I intentionally kept my thoughts and feelings to myself."

He smiled. "Yeah, actually you were pretty mean to me, but I still had a crush on you."

I raised an eyebrow. "Well, why didn't you say anything?"

"Because you were in a relationship, and when you weren't, I was."

I nodded playfully. "Well, yeah, I guess that's true."

Then he kissed me, and I felt so many sparks fly. We were and still are truly compatible. After that day we did not spend a day apart. We found a way to spend any free time we had together. He asked me to be his girlfriend on July 1st, 2020. We found love, and in September of 2020 he proposed. He took me to a place that that held deep significance for him, and then we stopped in Boerne, Texas, and walked the river. As we sat down to chat, an unexplainable urge came over me. I turned away from him and blurted out, "Do you think you could spend the rest of your life with me?"

Turning back around to face him, I saw him down on one knee, holding a ring. He said, "Yes, that's why I have this."

My excitement was instantaneous. "No way!"

With a grin from ear to ear he confidently asked, "Kaitlyn, I love you, will you marry me?"

Before he could even finish, I exclaimed, "Yes! Yes! Yes!"

As a first step toward our future together, we went to the courthouse and obtained our marriage license. Unlike the usual wait time, we were able to get it on the same day due to my military status. When we finally decided to share our wonderful news with our families, their reactions were truly heartwarming. Their faces lit up with pure happiness, and their excitement was contagious. They couldn't wait to be a part of our journey and offered their wholehearted support. Their enthusiastic response added an extra layer of joy to our special moment, making it even more unforgettable.

Our wedding seemed to approach in the blink of an eye. As October of 2020 rolled around, we found ourselves immersed in a beautiful ceremony surrounded by our closest family members. The one presiding over our union was none other than my stepdad, adding an extra layer of love to the occasion. Yes, it was a mere three months of dating that led us to this significant milestone of marriage. Yet our decision was rooted in a rock-solid certainty of our affection for one another and a deep commitment to withstand any challenges that might arise. The thought of being apart was, and still is, unfathomable.

Now, I'm not going to sit here and glorify everything like it was easy. My relationship with my husband did hit a rocky patch and I was devastated. I thought I was losing the love of my life. I thought that my manifestation of my long-lasting forever marriage was not coming true, and that I had made a naive wish. However, I forgot one key factor—my manifestation of love conquering all.

I will admit that we both made mistakes and getting past them was no easy feat. We ended up finding our way back to each other after a couple of months, and we were able to discuss all of the issues we were having and come to a resolution. We bounced back from the mistakes and came out on the other side even stronger. We worked on learning from each other and compromising to ensure that both of us were happy and healthy. I asked him if we could try to understand that it is us against the problem, not us against each other, and he agreed. Our love for one another was stronger than the problems we had faced. I believed it and told myself that love would be stronger than any obstacle for all of those years.

Prior to our challenging period, we had already begun trying for a baby. Dealing with repeated disappointment from negative pregnancy tests was tough, but we didn't give up. Despite our efforts, the negative test results persisted, Causing me to doubt my ability to conceive. The separation paused our plans, but when we resolved our issues, we knew it was time to try again.

For three months, we faced countless negative tests that wore down my hope of having a family. Then, unexpectedly, I found myself saying, "I AM pregnant," repeatedly. It was a feeling I couldn't explain but believed deeply.

After another discouraging month, I had a surprising positive result in May. Even though I hadn't intentionally focused on it, the act of manifesting my pregnancy seemed to work. In 2023, we welcomed our beautiful baby girl, Emily. Today, my heart is full of love and happiness, a testament to the journey we went through and the joy we've found.

I now know that manifesting is not bullshit. It took a few tries for me to believe it, but my persistence and dedication came through for me. Keeping your mind, heart, and company positive does wonders for your life. I also know that when a manifestation is spoken, it will come true with time and persistence. Things take time and it took me years to figure out how to attract all the good things in life. Manifest, Manifest, MANIFEST! The harder you work toward being positive, the better your environment will become. Keep the thoughts of not being good enough out of your mind. Feed your mind, heart, and soul with all of the good and it will come back to you in unimaginable ways. You are not alone in self-doubt; we have all been there. Work to extinguish the fires that negativity has built in your mind, and replace them with peace, like a gentle breeze on a sunny day.

If you are ever in a dark place, write down all the bad things you are thinking about and replace them on a separate sheet of paper with positive thoughts. Rip up and throw away the negative paper. Then stand in the mirror and look at yourself while repeating all of the kind words. Make it a mission to do this every day and you will see that change eventually. Learning these skills can change your life. Repeat the affirmations, "I AM __, I FEEL __, I HAVE __," and use specific words to turn your dreams into reality.

I know that at first you will have doubts and it is going to be hard to escape the depths of your learned negativity, but what's the worst that can happen? A negative thought creeps back in? It is going to take consistency and determination. However, if you work hard, stay persistent, and believe, you WILL see a change. Manifestation isn't a miracle; it requires effort, but the results can be incredible. Once you understand how to use the necessary skills, you'll be able to turn your desires into reality.

When faced with challenges, start by tackling something small. Instead of feeling overwhelmed by a messy house and not knowing where to start, change your mindset. Tell yourself, "Tomorrow, I'll clean up and have a neat house. A clean space makes me feel calm and happy." Or say, "Today, I'll clean my room, bathroom, and hallway. It'll help reduce my stress."

Likewise, if you're stuck in traffic because of an accident and running late for work, shift your perspective. Instead of just focusing on being late, remind yourself, "At least I'm safe and well."

Life's challenges can feel like a lot, but breaking tasks into smaller steps can make things easier. Doing this changes negative thoughts into positive ones, helping you manage stress and difficulties more effectively.

The phrase "look on the bright side" might seem cliché, causing us to react with a skeptical eye-roll. Yet buried within that common saying lies a valuable nugget of wisdom. In reality, those who offer this advice might be onto something profound. When faced with challenges, uncertainties, or even simple disappointments, taking a moment to shift our focus to the positive aspects can genuinely make a difference.

So, if you're unsure about where to start your journey toward creating a more positive mindset, consider embracing this simple yet powerful notion: looking on the bright side. It doesn't mean ignoring challenges or pretending that negative aspects don't exist; rather, it's about training your mind to acknowledge difficulties while also recognizing the potential for positive outcomes, growth, and learning.

By adopting this perspective, you're not engaging in a foolish way of thinking. Instead, you're equipping yourself with a tool that has the capacity to reframe your experiences. It's an approach that encourages resilience and fosters gratitude as well as a deeper appreciation for the complexities of life. So, as you embark on your journey toward a more positive outlook, remember that sometimes, even the most cliché pieces of advice can hold valuable truths.

In the upcoming chapter, you'll get the chance to start your own manifestation journey using practical steps. Manifestation isn't just a vague idea; it's a process that requires effort and practice. By following these steps, you'll learn how to align your intentions with actions to make your dreams come true.

These steps give you a clear path to effective manifestation. From setting clear goals to taking inspired actions, this toolkit will help you turn your desires into reality.

Remember, this isn't about instant results, but a continuous effort. Manifestation takes time and commitment. As you read the next chapter, be open to a new way of thinking and acting. These easy-to-implement steps will be your guide to unlocking your own power to shape your reality.

CHAPTER 2
CALL TO ACTION

If you find yourself standing at a crossroads in life, yearning for a substantial shift, I'm eager to introduce you to a roadmap that has profoundly impacted my own journey. The steps I've outlined in this chapter were crucial in steering the course of my life in a more positive and fulfilling direction. While your journey will undoubtedly be unique, my hope is that these insights can serve as a guiding light as you navigate your own transformation.

It's important to recognize that the process of transformation requires both sincere effort and unwavering commitment. As you delve into the following steps, I encourage you to approach them with an open heart and mind. This guide is a companion meant to support you on your journey toward self-discovery and growth.

Together, let's embrace the exhilarating adventure that lies ahead—a journey that promises to illuminate new possibilities and empower you to shape the future you desire.

Step 1: Acknowledging the Need for Change

Embarking on a journey of transformation invariably starts with a critical realization: recognizing the existence of an issue that warrants attention. This first step is a pivotal moment in which you take an honest look at your life, thoughts, habits, and circumstances and admit that something isn't quite right. It could be negative thought patterns that keep holding you back, the grip of anxiety that interferes with your daily life, the constant lure of distractions that hinder your productivity, or even the persistent tendency to procrastinate on important tasks.

This step requires a courageous self-analysis and a willingness to confront the aspects of yourself or your situation that may be hindering your progress or overall wellbeing. It demands an unwavering commitment to self-awareness, which in turn sets the stage for genuine growth and transformation.

Deciding to face these issues head-on, rather than ignoring or denying them, is an act of empowerment. It signifies your readiness to take charge of your life and make it better. It's like turning on the lights in a room that was previously dimly lit, allowing you to clearly see the corners that need cleaning and the changes that need to be made.

However, this step is not solely about identifying the problem. It's also about acknowledging the discomfort it brings and understanding that it doesn't align with the version of yourself you aspire to be. This acknowledgment lays the foundation for genuine change and sets the wheels in motion for the transformative journey ahead.

At its core, Step 1 entails taking a brave and honest look within, acknowledging the desire for change, and making a clear and unwavering commitment to addressing the issue at hand. It's about acknowledging that change is possible and that you have the power to shape your own path. This first step is not just a proclamation of intent; it's a pivotal moment that marks the turning point toward personal growth and transformation.

Step 2: Shift Your Thinking

In personal transformation, the power of our thoughts cannot be underestimated. This second step is about actively altering your thought process, a journey that might require time and persistent effort. The level of consistency you maintain in this endeavor holds the key to the ease of your transition. Just like practicing a skill over and over, the more regularly you engage in this process, the more natural and effortless it becomes.

Imagine your thoughts as a garden. Just as you cultivate and tend to a garden to ensure it flourishes, similarly, you need to nurture your thought patterns to promote positive growth. It's about replacing the "I can nots" with empowering "I cans." This shift might seem small, but its impact is profound.

If you're grappling with this step, it's perfectly okay to start small. Instead of letting self-limiting thoughts dictate your actions, you can challenge them by making small adjustments. For instance, consider a scenario where you're contemplating skipping the gym due to a to-do list that includes laundry, cooking, and cleaning. Rather than believing the idea that you "can't," reframe it by saying, "I'll first complete the chores, cook, and tidy up. Then, while the laundry is running, I'll take advantage of the time to follow a workout video."

By approaching things in this manner, you're not just changing your language; you're altering your entire perspective. Suddenly, the household tasks that might have felt hindering become stepping stones to achieving your fitness goals. This new mindset encourages you to manage your time more efficiently, ensuring that you create space for the activities you're genuinely passionate about.

This step underscores the importance of recognizing that our thoughts have a profound influence on our actions. It's a reminder that by nurturing a positive and growth-oriented mindset, you're setting yourself up for success in your transformative journey. While changing thought patterns might require patience, the rewards—a renewed sense of empowerment, a greater sense of control, and the realization that obstacles can be transformed into opportunities with a simple shift in perspective—are worth it.

Step 3: Transform Your Self-Perception

The next significant stride involves reshaping the way you view yourself. It's time to truly recognize the beauty within you. To begin, let's focus on altering the lens through which you perceive yourself.

Start by reflecting on any negative self-perceptions you might hold. Now, grab a piece of paper and switch these negatives for their positive counterparts. For instance, if you find yourself thinking, "I am unattractive," replace it with "I am beautiful." If the thought "I am unintelligent" arises, counter it with "I am smart," and so on.

Take that piece of paper with your newly formed positive affirmations and tape it to your mirror. As you go about your mornings, whether brushing your teeth or preparing for the day, look at your reflection and repeat these affirmations. This practice serves as a powerful tool for building your self-assurance, nurturing your confidence, and ultimately allowing your inner radiance to shine through.

Remember, transformation begins within. By actively replacing self-doubt with self-affirmation, you're planting the seeds of self-love and empowerment. This practice might seem simple, but its impact is profound. Over time, your perception of yourself will evolve, and you'll notice a positive shift in your self-confidence. So, embrace this step as a means to cultivate a more nurturing and loving relationship with the person who matters most—you.

Step 4: Music Therapy for Self-Positivity

In this step, we delve into the transformative power of music as a tool for cultivating self-positivity. It's truly remarkable how a single song can serve as a source of empowerment, confidence, and inner strength. When life presents its challenges and you find yourself feeling down or lost, turn to the healing embrace of musical therapy to uplift your mood.

The journey begins with the discovery of that one special song. It's the kind of melody that resonates with the deepest parts of your being, and its lyrics speak directly to your soul. These are not mere words; they are a wellspring of inspiration and encouragement.

When you press play on this chosen song, it's as though a switch is flipped within you. The music flows through your entire being, and suddenly, you stand a little taller, feel more capable, and fully embrace your inner beauty and strength. It's an experience of transformation that will leave you in awe of its potency.

What makes this musical remedy truly remarkable is its accessibility. Regardless of where you are or what you're going through, your chosen song is merely a click away. It becomes your secret weapon, your go-to lifeline during those moments when life's challenges threaten to overwhelm you.

Let listening to this empowering melody become a cherished ritual, a form of self-care that you hold dear. Allow it to serve as a constant reminder that within the notes and rhythms of the song, you can unearth the courage to confront any adversity, the confidence to surmount any obstacle, and the unwavering belief that you are beautiful and strong.

I wholeheartedly encourage you to embark on this journey of self-discovery through music. Find that song that resonates deeply with your heart and soul, the one that makes you feel as though you can conquer the world. And when life gets tough, let the music be your guiding light, lifting your spirits and reaffirming the incredible beauty and strength that reside within you.

Step 5: Harness the Power of Manifestation

Now, it's time to tap into the remarkable potential of manifestation. Begin by contemplating your deepest desires in life. These could range from aspirations that are within reach in the near future to dreams that may take time to materialize. Regardless of their timeline, it's crucial to pinpoint a specific, realistic date for each of your desires. For instance, you might say, "I intend to take my daughter to Disney for her second birthday in February 2025," or "I am committed to achieving financial stability and being debt-free by January 2024."

Once you've outlined your aspirations with clear timelines, the next step is to reframe them as "I wills." Transform each of your intentions into affirmative statements. Write down these "I wills" on a piece of paper. For example, "I will take my daughter to Disney for her second birthday in February 2025," or "I will achieve financial stability and be debt-free by January 2024." With this act, you've initiated the process of manifesting—a practice that brings your dreams into reality.

Manifestation is a process that involves aligning your thoughts, intentions, and actions with your desires. By declaring your goals as "I wills," you're sending a powerful message to yourself. This shift in mindset propels you toward a future where your goals are no longer distant possibilities, but tangible realities.

Remember, manifestation isn't merely about wishful thinking; it's about actively participating in the creation of your own destiny. As you write down your "I wills" and infuse them with determination, you're setting the stage for these aspirations to come to fruition. So, embrace this step as a gateway to turning your dreams into realities.

Step 6: Create Your Vision Board

Now, let's dive into vision boards, a powerful tool to amplify your manifestation journey. Begin by taking the paper on which you've written down your "I wills" and hang it on your wall. Next, find images that symbolize each of your manifestations. These images could be representations of your goals, aspirations, or the outcomes you're striving for.

Pin these selected images around your manifestation paper. As you do so, you're weaving together the power of words and visuals, creating a tangible representation of your dreams. This serves as a reminder of what you're working toward and reinforces that these aspirations are well within your reach.

The act of crafting a vision board is more than just the placement of images. It's about being able to view your intentions, desires, and aspirations together. Each image becomes a source of inspiration, urging you to stay committed to your goals.

By having your manifestations and visual representations in your line of sight, you're continuously reinforcing the connection between your dreams and your actions. This process encourages you to visualize yourself experiencing the outcomes you desire, instilling a sense of confidence and determination.

In essence, your vision board becomes a visual roadmap that guides you toward the reality you're envisioning. It serves as a daily reminder of your intentions and fuels your motivation to take steps that align with your aspirations. So, as you pin your images and words, enjoy the creative process and allow your vision board to serve as a powerful tool in transforming your dreams into your lived experiences.

Step 7: Take Action and Put in the Effort

Now that you've set your intentions, visualized your aspirations, and created your vision board, it's time to roll up your sleeves and get to work. This step is a pivotal reminder that for your dreams to transform into reality, action is necessary. You might declare intentions like, "I will have a million dollars in my bank account within two years." However, if you spend those two years lounging on the couch watching TV, your desire becomes unrealistic and out of reach.

The most important part of this step is recognizing that manifestation isn't a magic trick. It requires your active participation, effort, and commitment. Your intentions and dreams are seeds, and the work you put in serves as the nourishment that allows them to grow.

Think of it this way: Your actions and choices are the bridges between your current reality and the future you're envisioning. To bring your manifestations to life, you must step into the role of active participant in your own transformation. This might involve learning, planning, executing, and sometimes even pushing beyond your comfort zone.

The message of this step is clear: If you're determined to see your desires come to light, you must be prepared to invest the necessary time, energy, and effort. It's about aligning your actions with your intentions and using your vision board as a guide to steer you toward success.

Remember, the journey of transformation is an ongoing process that requires consistent dedication. By putting in the work, you're not only propelling yourself closer to your goals, you're also growing the sense of accomplishment that comes from knowing that you're actively shaping your own future. So, embrace this step as a call to action, a reminder that your efforts are the guiding force behind making your dreams your reality.

If you would like some more examples of manifestations, here are a few off of my current list:

Achievable Within 6 Months

This book, "Is Manifesting Bullshit?" is going to be an Amazon best seller by December of 2023.

Achievable Within a Year

I will have financial freedom and no debt by the end of 2024.

Achievable Within 5 Years

I will purchase a property in Texas with six houses to rent out and start making passive income by January of 2029. I will have no problems with my tenants and will have a trustworthy manager running the property.

All of these manifestations are attainable—I just have to work and the rest will fall into place. Following this, I will include examples of pictures I've used for my manifestations. If you resonate with these please feel free to use them.

As you come to the end of this guide, it's important to recognize that the journey of transformation you're embarking on is both a personal and empowering one. The steps outlined here are not just abstract concepts; they are practical tools that can guide you on a more fulfilling and positive path. While your experiences are uniquely yours, the principles and insights shared in this guide are meant to serve as a support on your journey of self-discovery and growth.

Embracing change and transformation requires effort and commitment, but the rewards are immeasurable. By acknowledging the need for change, shifting your thinking, transforming your self-perception, harnessing the power of manifestation, creating a vision board, and putting in the necessary effort, you're actively crafting the future you desire.

As you read through these pages, approach the material with an open mind and heart. Be receptive to new possibilities and insights that may resonate with your own experiences. Remember, this guide is not a rigid roadmap; it's a flexible tool that you can adapt and mold to your unique circumstances.

Your journey is a story that's still being written. Every moment, every choice, and every step you take contributes to your personal narrative. Embrace challenges as opportunities for growth, celebrate successes as milestones of progress, and seek connections with others who are on their own transformative paths.

Above all, remember that your journey is about more than just reaching a destination. It's about the strength you discover within yourself, the lessons you learn along the way, and the continuous growth you experience. Embrace the process creating a story that not only inspires you but also empowers others.

Your journey continues with each new day and each choice you make. Embrace the journey, and may it lead you to a life filled with purpose, joy, and the realization of your true potential.

Inspirational images chosen by Kaitlyn Chavez

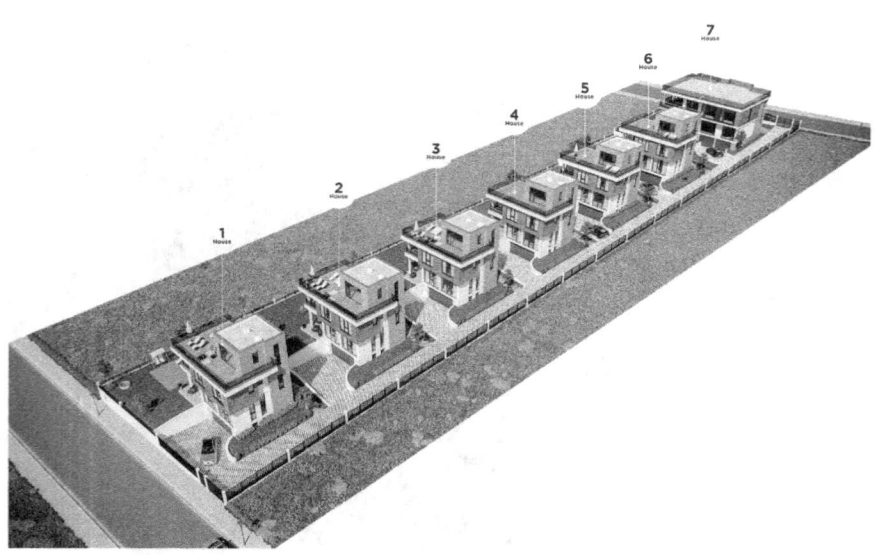

INTERVIEW WITH THE AUTHORS

Are you on the lookout for ways to infuse your life with greater positivity and creativity? Do you have a burning desire to manifest the life you've always envisioned? We're absolutely delighted to present you with an insightful interview for which we sat down with Angela Bell from She Rises Studios. During this engaging conversation, we delved into the depths of our manifesting journeys, offering a candid glimpse into our experiences and perspectives.

In this interview, we unravel the essence of manifesting, shedding light on how simple yet powerful techniques can serve as catalysts for nurturing positive thinking and setting forth on a transformative journey toward a life filled with purpose and fulfillment. Along the way, we unravel the web of common misconceptions surrounding manifestation, those subtle beliefs that often act as roadblocks on our path to realizing our true potential.

Through this captivating dialogue, we aim to provide you with practical wisdom and heartfelt insights that empower you to harness the profound potential of manifesting. By the time you've explored the depths of this inspiring interview, we're confident that your belief in the remarkable power of manifestation will have grown stronger, propelling you forward with renewed vigor and a heightened sense of possibility.

Angela

All right, so we are here with Cindy, Kaitlyn, and Kimberley, authors of *Is Manifesting Bullshit?* To get started, can you ladies tell me what manifesting means to you?

Cindy Witteman

In my view, manifestation is the act of transforming thoughts into actions. I believe that by effectively directing your thoughts and pinpointing your genuine dreams and desires, you lay the foundation for bringing them to life. Once you've identified these aspirations, taking proactive measures becomes an integral part of the manifestation journey.

Angela

Wonderful.

Kimberley Witteman

Manifesting to me is really thinking, believing, and feeling your true desires to bring them to your reality.

Angela

Awesome.

Kaitlyn Chavez

And manifesting to me is a mindset. It's a way to figure out what you truly want and then work toward that goal by becoming more positive and working to surround yourself with the things that you want.

Angela

Wonderful. What are some common techniques or practices that people can use to manifest their desires? What are some that you personally use?

Cindy Witteman

For me, writing is my go-to method. At various points in my life, I've faced moments of uncertainty about my desires. Sitting down to jot down ideas or simply allowing my thoughts to flow onto paper has been incredibly beneficial. This process has acted as a mental organizer, allowing my true aspirations to surface. Once I've identified what I truly want, I can then establish goals to work toward those desires. Writing serves as my primary tool for this purpose.

Kimberley Witteman

Mine is writing what I feel in relation to what I desire, as well as meditation to center myself and relax and calm my mind so I can focus on my true desires. Another thing that works for me is laying in bed before I go to sleep and thinking, feeling, and believing that I truly have what I desire.

Kaitlyn Chavez

And for me, one thing that I always have done is talk. Even if it's just talking to myself, looking at myself in the mirror and speaking to myself and creating those positive thoughts in my mind, telling myself what I am and what I am not. I also use visual aids; I am a very visual person. So creating a vision board always really helps because then I can picture myself doing whatever it is that I want with my life.

Angela

Amazing. I'm a big fan of mirror work as well. Kimberley, I wonder if you could just elaborate on one thing a little more. If someone says, "How do I feel as though I already have something I've never had before?" can you explain a little bit about how you do that or how you can get into that feeling, even though maybe you've never really experienced it?

Kimberley Witteman

Yes. It does take some work. What I always do is remember how I feel when I work really hard for something and I get it. That feeling of joy, feeling proud of yourself and what you've accomplished, feelings like that. Feel those in relation to the item that you desire. You can also try to counteract and correct the feelings that it will never happen, or that you don't have the thing you want. Feelings of joy, pride, and a sense of accomplishment really help me get into the mindset to manifest the things I desire.

Angela

Wonderful. Thank you. All right, can you explain the role that your beliefs, your personal beliefs, whether they're limiting or otherwise, and your mindset, have in the process of manifesting?

Cindy Witteman

I grappled with prolonged periods of self-doubt and self-sabotage, which significantly hindered my ability to manifest my desires. A major hurdle was my struggle to believe that I was deserving of what I yearned for. This obstacle held me back immensely. To overcome this, I dedicated myself to self-improvement, working on cultivating positive thinking and practicing gratitude for what I already had. As I honed the skill of appreciating my current blessings, I gradually realized that despite my self-imposed limitations, I was achieving quite a bit. Even as a single mother of four daughters, I managed to purchase and build a home tailored to our needs, while excelling in my career. This realization was a turning point, as I had been held back by my own self-doubt and failed to recognize my achievements.

Learning to be grateful for what I had made me realize my worth and strength. It showed me that with hard work, I can achieve anything I set my mind to.

Kimberley Witteman

I also struggled a lot with self-doubt, and I was very hard on myself, worried about everybody else instead of worrying about myself. I really do think that it's important to put yourself first, and feel the feelings that you need to feel to get yourself to the place that you need to be to manifest. If you block out those feelings, if you keep them in, if you don't talk about them, it just causes you to struggle mentally and prevents you from getting into the mindset. I really do feel that your emotions need to be validated, too. It can be either self-validation or validation from somebody else, depending on the person. Sometimes both are very good. Also, understanding that everything that you have, including the pen and paper that you write with or the thoughts in your head, whether positive or negative, are something to be grateful for.

Kaitlyn Chavez

From my experience in life, I have learned that if you have negative thoughts or surround yourself with negative people, the only outcome that can come from that is negative. But if you switch that mindset to a positive outcome and you truly believe that it's going to be positive, you're going to receive positive things in life. It's surrounding yourself with positive people and believing in positive things, including believing in yourself, that just completely changes your life from negative to positive.

Angela

Awesome. Do you ladies have any tools, podcasts, books, affirmations, YouTube videos, or anything that you listen to or read to help keep yourself in the attitude of gratitude or a positive mindset?

Cindy Witteman

Certainly, I've got a few recommendations. I recently read through *The Power of One More* by Ed Milette. I read it twice because it's all about taking action and teaching the value of giving one more effort. It's a book I really resonate with. Additionally, I've delved into *Think and Grow Rich* and *Into the Magic Shop*. And of course, *The Secret* crossed my path early in life. In fact, when I initially decided to explore this whole manifesting concept, I vividly recall gathering my daughters and showing them the movie version of *The Secret*, enthusiastically explaining our new manifesting journey. Looking back, they listened with a mix of patience and eye-rolling, probably thinking I'd gone a bit mad. So *The Secret* holds a special place. These are just a few books I genuinely love, as they've played a significant role in guiding my journey of manifestation.

Kimberley Witteman

For me, it was the movie *The Secret*. I watched that over and over again.

A couple of podcasts that I listen to are from James Van Prague. He talks a lot about manifesting and how to center oneself, and how meditation is not only humming and sitting crisscross, but meditation could also be sitting in a quiet room, calming your mind, listening to music. Meditation can happen in multiple different ways and I just love the fact that he goes into so much detail about manifestation and about certain things that most people don't know about.

Kaitlyn Chavez

For me it has always been music. I listen to a lot of self-love music and a lot of positive, good vibes music. Anything that makes you feel happy. And for those songs that are self-building songs, you want to sing them as loudly as you can and sing them as if you're singing them to yourself. And that helps build a lot of self-confidence. Something else that helps a lot is I watch a lot of TikTok videos, the positive ones. I'm a new mom, so the ones that are telling me, "Yes, this is hard, but you are a new mom and you're doing a great job," stuff like that really helps me build that self-confidence and positive mindset.

Angela

Wonderful. So why do you ladies think that so many people believe that manifesting is bullshit?

Cindy Witteman

Many people think manifesting is "bullshit" due to unrealistic expectations and misunderstandings. Some believe it's a magical fix without effort, leading to disappointment. Manifesting contrasts with traditional hard work approaches, making it seem disconnected. Misinformation adds to doubts. Fear of disappointment also plays a role. Overall, doubts stem from unrealistic beliefs and a lack of clarity about how manifesting works.

Kimberley Witteman

I feel like most people think manifesting is bullshit because they don't realize that there's a lot of work that goes into manifesting. It's not something that will come overnight and your ideas or things you desire have to be realistic. You can't manifest an elevator to the moon.

Kaitlyn Chavez

I think that people don't believe in manifesting simply because they put it into unrealistic terms and they see it as way too good to be true. People think manifesting is instead of working toward what they want, but manifesting is not just "I want something, I have it, and now it's in my hand." Once you get into writing down or picturing and feeling what you have, that's when your mindset starts to change and you start to work toward those goals.

Kimberley Witteman

Goals.

Kaitlyn Chavez

You could manifest like, "I'm going to be a millionaire in two years." But if you sit on your couch and do nothing to work towards that, then you're not going to become a millionaire. But if you say, "I'm going to become a millionaire in two years," and you go and you work your butt off, that's more realistic, and that can come.

Angela

Yeah, absolutely. I think a lot of people forget about that inspired action part, right? They think it's just sitting cross-legged and dreaming. There's inspired action involved. You all touched a bit on gratitude. What role does gratitude play in the manifesting process?

Cindy Witteman

Gratitude plays a pivotal role in the manifestation journey by acting as a powerful amplifier of positive energy. When you genuinely appreciate what you have, it shifts your perspective from focusing on lack to acknowledging abundance. This shift in mindset aligns your energy with the universe in a way that attracts more of the same positive experiences.

In essence, gratitude acts as a magnet that attracts positivity and abundance. By nurturing a grateful mindset, you create an environment conducive to manifesting your desires, as you're already in alignment with the energy you wish to attract.

Kimberley Witteman

Gratitude plays a huge role. When I started the manifesting part of my life, I was checking all other boxes but gratitude. And the more

I tried and tried to manifest, the harder it got. Once I watched *The Secret* for the second time, after watching it with my mom when I was younger, I realized that manifesting has a lot to do with gratitude. You have to be grateful for the food you eat, the pen and paper you have to write with. Little things mean the most, because it's the little things people don't necessarily think about. It's really good to write down everything you're grateful for and center yourself around those things.

Kaitlyn Chavez

Gratitude is very important when it comes to manifesting, because if you do not show that you're grateful for what you already have, you'll never be grateful for things that you get. So, say I manifest a 75-inch flat-screen TV. That's what I want in my house, and I get it. Well, I'm not going to be grateful for it. In the end, it's not going to work out. And the more you're grateful for things, the more things come into your life that you are manifesting.

Angela

Amazing. Okay, one final question. And Cindy, I'm going to direct this to you, but Kaitlin and Kimberley feel free to jump in here as well. I myself have eight-year-old twins, a boy and a girl, and I've tried speaking to them about manifesting and visualization and how they can control and create their own reality and stuff like that. And they roll their eyes at me, obviously, and think that I'm crazy and kind of tune me out. So, at what stage were your daughters open to the idea, or what had to happen for the idea to be plausible for them? For other parents out there looking to help their children with this, is there anything you did specifically? How do you recommend approaching it with our kids?

Cindy Witteman

It's incredible how my older daughters and I have grown through challenges together. They've witnessed my journey through financial struggles, like sharing a single-dollar cheeseburger, to embracing abundance through manifestation. This path has shown them the true power of manifestation firsthand.

My girls and I often chat about techniques like changing mindsets and practicing gratitude. However, my youngest, Kaylie, at 12, is more skeptical. She hasn't experienced the earlier struggles, so she sees our lives as always having been abundant.

My advice to parents is to share your journey and insights, but allow your kids to find their own way. While we wish to guide our kids, they'll learn when the time is right. Each child's journey is unique, and they'll grasp the concept of manifestation in their own time.

Angela

Yeah, they will. Kaitlin, Kimberley, did you guys want to add anything?

Kaitlyn Chavez

Yes. I will say that growing up, kids learn by trial and error. You can give them the information all you want, but it's going to go in one ear and out the other until they're ready to receive that information. That's exactly how it was with me. Mom tried to explain it to me so many times, and I was like, yeah, Mom, whatever. I even wrote about that in my chapter. But when I actually started, I was here in Great Falls, Montana, I had moved away from all of my family. My husband and I were stationed here. And so, I'm here by myself trying to figure out things, and I was just in a super low place, and I was basically like, "Okay, I need to do something to change." I started implementing manifesting because it's something that I can control and something that I can do to change my life. And slowly but surely, it started to work. The more and more I worked at it, the more and more I poked at doing the things that I wanted to do, the better my life became. And I'm still growing every day, I'm still learning new things every day, but it is just a process of trial and error. You have to work for it.

Angela

Awesome. Alright ladies, thank you very much for sharing all of that with me. Thank you.

In conclusion, our conversation with Cindy, Kaitlin, and Kimberley shed light on the multifaceted world of manifesting. Each author offered a unique perspective on how they interpret and practice manifestation in their lives. From transforming thoughts into actions to channeling positive emotions, the journey of manifesting is one that requires dedication, self-awareness, and the ability to shift one's mindset.

As discussed, manifesting goes beyond wishful thinking; it involves aligning beliefs, thoughts, emotions, and actions toward a desired outcome. By incorporating techniques such as writing, visualization, and affirmations, individuals can actively participate in their own manifestation journey. Moreover, the role of gratitude is a powerful force in attracting positivity and abundance. The authors emphasized the importance of appreciating even the smallest blessings, as gratitude acts as a catalyst for manifesting desires.

The skepticism around manifesting, as addressed, often stems from misconceptions and a failure to recognize the practical efforts required. The authors dismantled this notion by highlighting the necessity of inspired action and realistic goals. By understanding that manifesting involves a partnership between intention and effort, individuals can harness the true potential of this practice.

In the context of guiding children on their own manifesting journeys, the authors offered valuable insights. Sharing personal experiences and lessons can lay the groundwork, but allowing children to find their unique paths is equally essential. Patience and understanding were echoed as key approaches to introducing young minds to the power of manifesting.

Ultimately, this interview reaffirms that manifesting is a dynamic process that intertwines beliefs, actions, and emotions. Through shared experiences and practical advice, Cindy, Kimberley, and Kaitlyn inspire us to approach life with intention, positivity, and the belief that we have the power to shape our own realities. Whether it's through writing, visualization, or simply fostering an attitude of gratitude, the principles of manifesting serve as a roadmap to unlocking our full potential and creating a life aligned with our true desires.

Closing Remarks from the Authors

Thank you for spending your time reading this book. We hope you have enjoyed it. As women who have learned how to manifest properly and the authors of this book, we would like to help you on your journey into abundance. We offer vision board and manifestation workshops. You can choose to attend a group workshop or a 1-on-1 session if you would prefer to keep it private. Please see below for links to schedule. If you have questions or would like to learn more about the authors, please see their individual contact information below.

Schedule a FREE 1-on-1 chat with the author of your choice by using the following links:

Cindy Witteman:
https://calendly.com/cindywitteman/20min

Kimberley Witteman:
https://calendly.com/nikkikimmy15/30min?month=2023-08

Kaitlyn Chavez:
https://calendly.com/kaitlyn5498mail/30min?back=1&month=2023-08

Author Contact Information:

Cindy Witteman

Primary Email Address:
Founder@DrivingSingleParents.org
https://linktr.ee/cindy.witteman

501©3 Nonprofit
Driving Single Parents Inc.
Website: DrivingSingleParents.org
Email: Info@DrivingSingleParents.org
Facebook Page: https://www.facebook.com/DrivingSingleParents

Little Give
with Cindy
Little Give TV Show
Website: LittleGive.com
Email: Cindy@LittleGive.com
https://linktr.ee/cindy.witteman
Wanna be a guest?
Pre-Show Interview Scheduling Link:
https://calendly.com/cindywitteman/20min
Little Give TV Show Facebook Group Link:
https://m.facebook.com/groups/743349997160678/?ref=share

CF Views LLC

Website: CFViews.com

Email: Info@CFViews.com

-Nonprofit Startup Coaching

-Life & Confidence Coaching

-Advertising

-Purchase books Authored by Cindy Witteman

https://linktr.ee/cindy.witteman

Facebook Page:

https://www.facebook.com/profile.php?id=100089195777362

Kimberley Witteman

Email Address:
Website:
https://cfviews.com/kimberley-witteman
Linktree:
https://linktr.ee/kimberley.witteman?utm_source=linktree_admin_share
Scheduling Link:
https://calendly.com/nikkikimmy15/30min?month=2023-08

Kaitlyn Chavez

Email Address:
Chavez.Kaitlyn2020@gmail.com
Website:
https://cfviews.com/kaitlyn-chavez
Linktree:
https://linktr.ee/kaitlynchavez?utm_source=linktree_admin_share
Scheduling Link:
https://calendly.com/kaitlyn5498mail/30min?back=1&month=2023-08